# Waterloo Boy
## Some Macclesfield Memories

by

## Geoffrey Hunter

**Churnet Valley Books**

Published by

**CHURNET VALLEY BOOKS**

43 Bath Street
Leek
Staffordshire
01538 399033

© Geoffrey Hunter and Churnet Valley Books
1996

ISBN 1 897949 23 5

Printed in Great Britain by the Ipswich Book Company, Suffolk

For
Paul, Lorraine and Adèle
with love

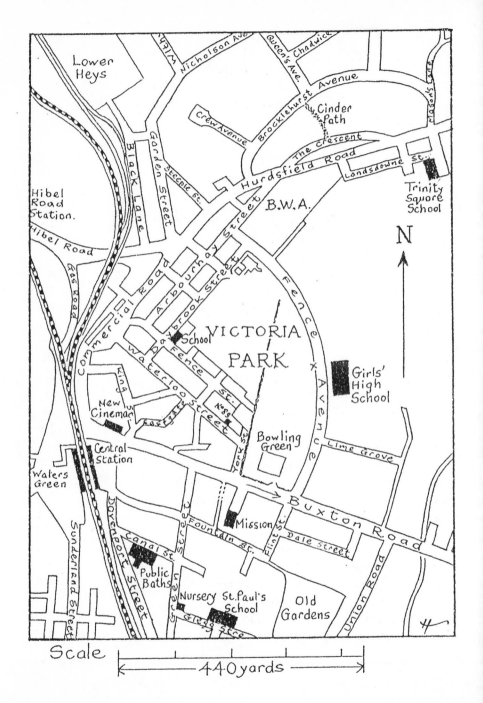

Scale

|← 440 yards →|

# Contents

Introduction      Doug Pickford
Acknowledgements
Prologue

# Introduction

Many Maxonians will recall the Old Macclesfield articles in the Macclesfield Express - they were articles that I had great pleasure in being associated with for many years - not least because I met so many lovely Macclesfield people in the process.

I so well remember one morning a few years ago when I was at my desk and the receptionist telephoned through to inform me that "a gentleman named Mr Hunter" would like to see me. In strode a tall elder statesman of the town. His rich Macclesfield tones were a joy to hear as he related one story and then another about Macclesfield of years long gone. He then asked me if I would consider publishing an article he had written about his childhood days in the Waterloo Street area of Macclesfield. He showed me several foolscap pages written in a fine copperplate hand.

They were a joy. There was no hesitation on my part - they had to be printed, and no sooner had the first one come 'hot off the press' than the whole town was abuzz.

Geoffrey Hunter, the 'Waterloo Boy' of the series, had captured everyone's imagination and had re-kindled many, many memories by the tales of his 1930s childhood from going to the cinema to watch his idols of the silver screen to his lists of the many people he could recall who were part of the community. They were as much a part of Macclesfield as oatcakes and silk.

Geoffrey Hunter's rich turn of phrase and talent for recalling the finest details of the past are something that he has, I know, had pleasure in sharing - and which countless thousands have received pleasure from.

Geoffrey became a firm friend of mine. He is a wonderful man and I am delighted that he has decided to write this book. He has encapsulated not only his own young days during the 1930s and 40s in Treacle Town but he has also compiled an important source of historical fact written in his unique way. I have no hesitation in recommending this book to the reader; I know everyone will be thrilled, delighted and entertained. This has been a labour of love for Geoffrey and I know he wishes to share it with you all. God bless him!

**Doug Pickford**
Editor of the Macclesfield Express
(later Express Advertiser) 1972 -1995

# Acknowledgements

This book would not have been written without the sustained enthusiasm, encouragement and practical help of my esteemed friend, Doug Pickford, former editor of the Macclesfield Express. His generosity to me has known no bounds.

My thanks also to dear Claire Crosbie who has accompanied me every inch of the way on this nostalgic journey, and whose dedication and perception have surely enhanced the finished product.

In addition to the support I have received from the members of my own family, I am grateful also to the many people - far too numerous to mention individually - who have responded so favourably since I began writing articles of my early life for the Macclesfield Express in October 1992. Several of those articles, incidentally, combined with much material new to the reader, comprise this book.

The warm and repeated encounters with the Macclesfield public during the past few years have added to my understanding of times past, and in this regard I am happy to acknowledge the contributions of John Sutton, Hubert Glazebrook, Norman Sutton, Ronald Tomkinson, Roy Booth and John Pimblott.

G.H.
October 1996

**A fine photograph of 'Annie' taken at the end of the Great War just prior to her decision to seek a new career as a silk weaver.**

*Photo: Bullock Bros, Macclesfield*

# Prologue

Young Annie had every reason to be pleased with herself. Following a short period as a trainee mental nurse at Parkside Hospital, she had been 'placed' in the Uplands block, opened just over a year previously. A genteel appendage to the main hospital, it catered for the mental welfare of well-to-do paying guests or, as Macclesfield folk would term them, 'the better end'.

Uplands was a splendid addition to the Parkside complex. Fine bathroom facilities and potted plants everywhere impressed on Annie a refined ambience her endeavours were intended to match! Should any staff member fall short in any way, Matron, an awesome matriarch, was there with her all-seeing eyes to ensure things were done to the standard of her bidding. Despite the strictness of the regime, Annie was happy to be so chosen and almost wholly content in those early days.

This war situation did tend to put a cloud over things, though. Strange business about that Archduke chap Ferdinand and his wife being shot in that distant and unpronounceable place. One didn't care to hear of anyone being shot, of course, but why war? Still, Mr Asquith and the rest must know what they are doing and anyway, the general view is that it should all be over in a few weeks and then everything in the garden will be rosy.

Annie was in the thick of her duties mid-morning one Saturday when she received the instruction to report to Matron's quarters. Naturally uneasy with this command, Annie hastily checked her appearance and smoothed herself down (mustn't keep Matron waiting) and presented herself with a light tap on Matron's door. Given the call to enter, she bobbed a quick curtsy as Matron rose from her settee. Annie noted a softness, foreign to the normal severity, in Matron's expression and was reassured.

"Nurse," said Matron, "I need help from someone I can trust." Annie warmed to this undisguised tribute. "Later today," continued Matron, "I am to be visited by a very old and esteemed friend and since the visit entails a fairly long journey I have decided to make a special effort and prepare a meal for the two of us in my own apartment. Accordingly, I have made a list of items I shall require from town and also the various shops where I wish these purchases to be made. You understand?"

"Yes, mum."

"Here is the list. You will note that your first call will be at Mr Potts' the poulterer in Chestergate - opposite the moving pictures place. You will get a fine bird there at a fair price. Tell Mr Potts that I require a plump little chicken with ample meat on it for two. Pay for it there and then but ask Mr Potts to put a 'sold' ticket on it and to save it for you to collect on your way back here. No point in taking the fowl for an unnecessary walk!

"Between times you can get the other things from the shops I've listed. If a particular shop hasn't what I require, use your initiative and acquire wisely from elsewhere but be sure to return with everything I've asked for. All right? Good. Here's your basket and there's a guinea. Go right away, and thank you."

It proved to be a pleasant chore for Annie to perform as she savoured the Saturday morning bustle of Chestergate, the market place and Mill Street, and in due course everything Matron had asked for was delivered to her. That should have been the last of Annie's involvement in the episode of the Matron's friend. However, at 7.30 in the evening of the same day Annie was once again summoned to Matron's rooms.

"Nurse, I have just received disappointing news. The full story need not concern you but I am afraid the friend I expected will not now be visiting me after all. The meal I am preparing is nearing completion and since you have contributed towards its preparation I wish you to share it with me. If you will return here at 8 o'clock, I will have the satisfaction of knowing that something good has been salvaged from this unhappy situation."

Shortly afterwards, therefore, Annie (who in the short time available to her had gone to great pains to make herself as presentable as possible) was admitted to Matron's quarters for the fourth time that day. The table was set tastefully for two and Annie was asked to take her seat. Soon the meek and the mighty sat facing each other, a steaming plate before each.

"Eat up!" commanded Matron, as her own knife and fork commenced their attack on her inspired repast.

An initial hesitancy on Annie's part conveyed itself almost immediately to Matron.

"Something the matter, nurse?" she asked.

"Well - er -"

"Speak up, nurse, I won't eat you! There is quite sufficient on my plate to satisfy my appetite. What is it?"

"Well, mum," said Annie carefully, "I'm most grateful to you, I'm sure, for inviting me here, but - but..."

Matron's attitude softened. "My dear girl," she said gently, "do feel

10

free to speak."

"Well, mum, it really is a beautiful dinner, it really is, but..."

"Go on," coaxed Matron.

"Well, if I'm to be perfectly honest with you, mum, I do believe I would get the greatest pleasure from this meal if I were able to enjoy it on my own, in my own room. I've no wish to cause offence mum, I'm sure, and if -"

"But of course, I should have known," said Matron generously, as full realisation of Annie's discomfort registered with her. "Far from causing any offence I think you are a very sensible young lady. Your wish to derive the fullest pleasure from the meal is mine also. Let me find you a cover for your plate and a cloth to keep everything warm. Here we are, this dish will do perfectly and this clean tea-towel will keep it all nice and cosy. Pick up your cutlery - I'll open the door for you - Now, off you go!"

That story of Annie's is a true story and it appears to indicate that she was set fair for a satisfying career in mental nursing. Nursing duties in those days combined a high degree of physical hard work as well and Annie was not found wanting. But she was also a deeply caring young woman and found it difficult to cope emotionally at times as she shared her charges' troubles, confusion, frustration and anguish. The final straw came when one of the elderly patients took her own life. Annie was devastated by this tragedy and made the decision to choose less-stressful employment. She took her leave to pursue a more contented and remunerative future in the silk factories of Macclesfield.

Had she not done so it is unlikely that she would ever have met Tom and in that event, the story you are about to read, dear reader, could not have been told.

**Girls in Mill Street School playground gathered to witness the eclipse in 1927**

# Chapter One
## A total eclipse

A total eclipse of the sun occurred on June 29th, 1927. Not witnessed in Britain in the previous 200 years, the north of England provided a good vantage area and the people of Macclesfield had mixed feelings of the silent darkening of the sky on this eventful day. Some stayed indoors, fearful that the world was coming to an end. Others congregated about town, a large number choosing to lie on the grassy slope below Sparrow Park, eager not to miss this rare phenomenon.

My mother was indoors that day, as apprehensive as the rest, in a room above the shop at 87 Mill Street, but it was to a son of a different spelling to which she gave her full consideration, for she gave birth to me on that day.

The shop in question, a three-storey building with considerable 'depth' behind its frontage has recently been 'done up' as the locals term refurbishment, and is now an attractive fresh food and wine emporium.

I know that in 1910 the premises had been the Royal Oak Inn but what type of shop it was seventeen years later when I exercised my lungs for the first time in one of the rooms above, I cannot say. My parents probably had little to do with the shop anyway, since access to their private quarters was gained via a door in an alley at the side of the building. The alley is there to this day. I was Mother's third son and fourth child and in descending order of age my siblings were Eileen, Tony and Vincent and there were eighteen months to two years between each of us.

They were hard times, as our accommodation indicated, and quite how my parents coped up to the time of my birth and immediately after it, I cannot think. My mother, Annie, was the breadwinner at all times - confinements apart - whereas my father, Tom, was employed fitfully and was glad of any work that came his way. He was a Preston man and he and his sister had been orphaned early in life and raised in an orphanage. Despite this inauspicious start in life he possessed a strong mathematical and literary ability.

In her teens my mother had been a nurse at Parkside Hospital and had earned responsibility but eventually chose to leave that employment and learn the art of silk weaving, becoming highly proficient and sought after by local manufacturers. My maternal grandmother, Granny Talbot, used to tell the story of one Friday evening of those days when her daughter arrived home on the heels of her stepfather and placed her opened wage packet on the table. Gazing at the packet's contents in amazement her stepfather said ruefully,"Well, this is a rum 'ow-d'you-do - dowghter comin' 'ome wi' more money that 't' faither!" As he was also a silk weaver his surprise and indignation was understandable.

Just who looked after us children when my father was in work I cannot say; Eileen was a little mother, of course, and it is possible that even in those early days use was made of Glegg Street nursery, a facility which was to prove a considerable boon to the family in following years.

Nothing shrinks space in the home more than successive children, and with my arrival on the scene the next few months served to strengthen the desire for more room and a more traditional family home. An application to Macclesfield Corporation produced a sympathetic response and my parents were allocated a newly-built house on Chadwick Terrace, Hurdsfield Estate.

This council house proved to be a non-blessing in pristine disguise for, once installed, Vincent, who was approaching his third birthday at the time, became unwell with a persistent cold and despite medical treatment his condition worsened over the next several weeks and eventually he was diagnosed as suffering from pneumonia. The family physician, Dr Marshall, Park Green Surgery, was firm in his conviction. "It's the house!" he exclaimed. "It's new and it is still drying out and is not suitable habitation for young children. You must move - and quickly." An exchange of homes was rapidly arranged, and soon the family was ensconced at 89 Waterloo Street, and it was at that home that I would witness and retain my first remembrance of life.

I was about a year old when the move to Waterloo Street was made so I can remember nothing of my early life there. At the outset, both Eileen and Tony were sent to Trinity Square School. Vincent's recovery was slow, as was indicated when he commenced his education at the same school a year later than normal. At some point, though, both Vincent and I were in day-care at Glegg Street nursery. A fine family house and a first-class establishment, access to the nursery was by a side door in Green Street which led to the back of the house where cover for prams was available.

In 1929 Leslie was born and in the Spring of 1931 Dorothy made her appearance. The pattern seemed to be to have two children at the nursery at any given time. Following Dorothy's birth in the run-up to my fourth birthday and the beginning of my schooling I stayed at home and was looked after by my father. It was at this point that I began to display a hint of artistic flair. I would pass the time sketching soldiers in a variety of poses with rifles and cannon, and cut out these figures and their weapons with a small pair of scissors. I had a good mental picture of such things as lead soldiers and their arsenal were commonplace as toys at that time and I considered there was nothing remarkable in what I was doing. Mother thought differently. "Instead of finding all these paper soldiers on the floor each time I come home, each morning before I go to work I will mix you a little flour-paste in a cup," she said, "then you can stick your soldiers on each side of the mantlepiece and I'll clean them off when you're in bed each night."

From then on for some period each day, war was declared with each side of the mantlepiece in conflict with the other.

Waterloo Street was a very long and straight gradient paved in stone sets throughout its length and extending in a south-easterly direction from Commercial Road, climbing fairly steeply at first and then gradually, for something approaching 300 yards until it ended at the top with a high stone wall bordering Victoria Park in York Street. York Street apart, five other streets led off from Waterloo Street. Daybrook Street was on the left about a quarter of the way up. At halfway Princess Street turned off acutely to the right followed quickly by Eastgate on the same side and shortly afterwards by Dicken Street on the left and Davies Street - often referred to as the 'Dunbar' - at an obtuse angle, opposite.

From this point on the final 100 yards of the left-hand side of the street and the yard behind the houses was what I might term 'my patch', commencing at the off-licence, number 67, on the corner of Dicken Street. My earliest recollection is of the off-licence being kept by the Ripleys who had an Airdale dog large enough to be fitted with a saddle; and not too long after that by the Lomases who had a sweet stall in the Waters Green market each Saturday, a stall cocooned in a rich aroma of sweet mintiness. The corner on which the shop stood was a popular gathering point for us youngsters. Not only was the shop's main window a lure, containing a good selection of sweets, but the corner was furnished with a gas lamp which, allied to its nocturnal virtue, served as a climbing frame for the energetic amongst us.

Names which come to mind in my stretch of the street were the Topliffes at about number 73. Their daughter, May, several years older than me, had been born disabled and spent much of her time, her legs encased in irons and leather straps, sitting at the open door dispensing cheerfulness to all who passed by. Mr Sam Norbury and family were at number 77. The Norbury's had two daughters, Joyce and Irene and a young lad, George. At 83 were the Rileys with grown-up children Jim, Florrie and Elsie; at 87, Mrs Rose and son Maurice (who married Florrie Riley at a later date). Then came our house followed by the Bracegirdles at 91 - they boasted a wireless set, and 93 was occupied by the Sherratts who had several girls, Ivy being the closest to my age. The Hills and son Donald were at 95, Laura Buxton at 97, the Suttons with son Norman at 99. There is a gap in my memory for the next two houses but Miss Smith lived in the top-most house, number 105.

A point worthy of mention is that the Sherratts moved to 17 Hibel Road in the mid-30s and conducted a thriving taxi business from that address for a good number of years. Mr Albert Gaskell and his young bride replaced them at number 93.

At the top right-hand corner of the street, facing Miss Smith's house was the Waterloo Inn, number 78, the landlord being Mr Lou Bradshaw. The Bradshaw's may have had plural children but I can recall only daughter Margaret.

Four doors down from the pub were the Beards with daughters Amy and Mildred and son Eric, closely followed by the Daniels, with sons Brian and Keith, the Stevensons (Geoffrey was the eldest son), the Fish family with son John at number 60, the Glazebrooks with daughter Annie and son Hubert at 58, Minnie Dean at 56 and Mrs Clark's shop at 54, on the corner of Davies Street.

Mrs Clark's shop window was not as alluring to me as Ripley's across the way, her line of sweets being nothing like as comprehensive. There were swaggering dicks (humbug rock with a brown spiral feature), chocolate coconut twists, jaw-strengthening licorice sticks, flattened at one end, marshmallow cones, Barratt's sherbet fountains and dabs and their open-ended packets of ten sweet cigarettes, reddened at the end, all at a ha'penny each. There were bars of Toblerone in their distinctive triangular boxes, but since these retailed at fourpence each it remained a confection beyond my wildest dream.

A good selection of bottled boiled sweets were also on offer at a ha'penny an ounce. True, the price stated on each bottle was two pence per quarter, but for us youngsters the exchange rate mechanism was seldom more than a ha'penny. Nothing, it seemed, was ever thruppence a quarter and with good reason, since one ounce sales had to be catered for. The next stage up was fourpence per quarter for such sweets as fruit bon-bons and Uncle Luke's cough tablets which were unwrapped and dusted with white powder to prevent them sticking together in the jar. A bottle of Camp coffee had a regular spot in the left of the window and a few cakes completed the display. Dad would send me here for his Gold Flake cigarettes which cost sixpence for ten - at a time, mark you, when there were 240 pence in the pound.

It was a jolly good shop for the area. In addition to basic foodstuffs there was a homely offering: firewood, and firelighters with a pungent smell, boot polish, Zebo in its black and orange striped tins for black-leading grates, Seidlitz powders and a variety of Stothert's patent medicines and ointments - castor oil, cough remedies, Indian brandy, syrup of figs, rubbing oils, corn plasters, etc. For those desirous of a really 'moving' experience there were Beecham's pills, reputedly 'worth a guinea a box'. There was a good sale for the ingenious and aptly-named 'bachelor buttons'. These were round, hollow, metal time-savers designed to eliminate the need for needle and thread. Enamelled black, these buttons were sold on cards together with a similar number of flanged studs. The studs were pushed through the back of clothing and then forced, with pressure, through the back of each button, press-stud style. The flange on the stud ensured the two parts stayed together permanently and they were ideal for men's trousers and overalls.

The shop's sales also placed strong emphasis on goods to keep home and appearance clean: rubbing stones and donkey stones for beautifying doorsteps, buckets and mops, brushes and shovels and washday goods of soap, starch, dolly blue and bleach. Our choice of soap was invariably Fairy; two chunky green blocks per packet, each embossed with the trade mark, Baby Hedley. One packet end was printed with two coupons, each worth a farthing, and these were always redeemed at the shop for sweets by us kids.

High on our list of purchases were Oxo cubes. A hot drink of Oxo and a slice of bread was a fairly frequent treat at our house and the nearest we ever came to having a supper. At a penny apiece each cube came in its own thin-carded box and these boxes could be saved, flattened for storage, and exchanged for gifts. Two footballs came our way from this scheme. At a later date this shop was taken over by Emmy Birtles.

A view from Dicken Street looking across Waterloo Street showing the full length of Davies Street with a Buxton Road Almshouse in the background. Taken just prior to demolition, this photograph shows Mrs Clark's former shop in the 1930s - later also owned by Emmy Birtles.

## Chapter Two
## My streets and neighbours

Moving further down Waterloo Street from Mrs Clark's shop, having crossed the opening of Davies Street, were two houses, numbers 52 and 50 with a small fenced-in frontage sharing the space between Davies Street and Eastgate with Fence Sunday School. In one of these houses lived the Browns whose daughter Kathleen was my age. I have an idea another child arrived later. I was in awe of the Browns. I regarded them as being 'posh'. Well, their home had the railings for one thing (a surprising feature of ostentation in our street, I always thought) and for another, Mrs Brown was a lady with such a natural stately bearing I likened her to a duchess!

We attended Fence Sunday School in the early years but later became affiliated to Daybrook Street Mission instead, perhaps because Daybrook incorporated a Band of Hope class on Monday evenings, which was quite good fun. Between Eastgate and Princess Street was situated Lancaster's newsagents shop which advertised Stephens' Ink prominently in its windows together with stationery items. Mrs Lancaster had two sons, Ronald and Graham. Theirs was an extremely successful newspaper business but not, I felt, a shop window to catch the eye.

A few yards further down still, on the corner of Princess Street was Pitcher's shop. A good mixed shop it was too, being grocer, greengrocer, confectioner, tobacconist - you name it. As I think of Pitcher's shop I am reminded of Christmas for invariably with the approach of the festive season, displayed in the window would be several cotton-wool 'snow' models containing raffle numbers and hidden prizes. These creations were ideal for family parties and held great fascination for me. Also, this shop always had a fine array of cakes on display. Mrs Pitcher - in my mind's eye I can see her now - had charge of the shop in the main. Her husband was employed by the North Western Road Car Company as a driver. They had a daughter, Nora, who developed into a fine soprano singer and subsequently married into the Macclesfield shoe family, Rose. Nor was Nora the only up-and-coming songstress in the area. Young Muriel Ward and Winifred Bracegirdle, some years older, who lived in Dicken Street within yards of each other, both also earned vocal popularity in later years.

Having just mentioned one Christmas display I am tempted to tell the tale of another and I beg leave to digress briefly from my journey down

Waterloo Street and tell you of Christmas 1930, when I was three and a half years old. I wandered, unchaperoned, to Commercial Road at the bottom of my street early one evening. The route was well illuminated with gas lamps and would not have been considered hazardous for a small child in those times. Having spent some time admiring the Xmas display in Mr Bob Ashton's shop on the corner of Fence Street, I was drawn by curiosity across Commercial Road to the pork butcher's shop of Mr Albert Kirk, which was ablaze with light. What a shock I got! Right across the window and facing me as I looked in was a row of pigs heads, about eight of them, each with an orange stuck in its mouth! I had never seen anything so bizarre in my short life and I was greatly disturbed by the incongruity of it all. Particularly distressing was that, since the pigs mouths had been prised open to accommodate the oranges, they appeared to be grinning when, clearly, they had nothing to smile about at all!

But, as I return to my Waterloo Street theme, I have little more to add. Only one more shop remained in the street, a grocer's on the corner of Daybrook Street, kept by Mrs Smith. By my reckoning this was number 17 and almost opposite her shop, at number 16, was the house that had been the Wheatsheaf pub, still outwardly displaying signs of its former trading days. Names I recall in this lower part of the street are Clarke, Booth, Ratcliffe, Weaver, Hulse, Cotterill and Stanway. There were, of course, other shops in the vicinity which played an important role in our family life. In the small cluster of shops opposite the Almshouses on Buxton Road, our constant butcher, Mr Devonport was situated. Through the years he supplied the means for our traditional Sunday roast, plus sausages, liver, and other incidentals throughout each week. Also in this short row of shops was Savage's grocer's which had a special line in boiled ham topped with golden bread crumbs and carved on the bone. This tasty offering was also the celebrated line of Pitcher's shop in my street, and of Mr Harrison whose little shop was in Flint Street, just off Buxton Road. The contest for best was a close thing, but my discerning mother gave her vote to Mr Harrison.

My favourite sweet shop was on Buxton Road facing York Street. Crowder's shop had only a small frontage with a little railed area in front of the window. It was chock-a-block with goodies. Mr & Mrs Crowder were the most handsome little couple, each with the kindliest countenance and I was happy to take my ha'pennies there. Later in the 30s they moved to Hurdsfield Road and continued their business life as drapers.

Davies Street was the route to take from our home when a visit to the lower Buxton Road Co-op was made, which was most days of the week. As one entered Davies Street from Waterloo Street, early on the left lived Mr & Mrs Sam Goodier and their daughter Kathleen. In due course they were to be blessed with another daughter, Jean, who as a toddler, might well have been dubbed 'Britain's answer to Shirley Temple'. Gorgeous little thing! Roughly opposite lived Mr & Mrs Ernest Farrow and their sons Gordon and Bill. Curiously enough, in later years both Mr Goodier and Mr Farrow would take, in their turn, the off-licence. Further along on the left lived the Gregorys. They had daughters Betty, and May, my age, and a year or two later, Brian. I have retained a memory of young Brian, resplendent in the finest cowboy outfit I ever did see! At the end on the left, the Sherratts, with daughters Gladys and Peggy and sons Albert and Eric, had a fair-sized yard.

At this point Davies Street ended and, I am informed on good authority, became the Dunbar, as it narrowed and meandered uneasily past Ben Cook's builders' yard into Buxton Road with Barnett's sweet shop on the left corner close to the old Bull Inn. Across the road was the Co-op where we bought our 'loose' best butter at one shilling and sixpence per pound, $7\frac{1}{2}$p in today's currency. Farm cobbs, a favourite bread item of ours, were seven for sixpence. Our 'divi' number was 3098. Close at hand was Livesey's chip shop with fish, chips, fritters, peas, beans, tripe and mineral waters on sale. The Liveseys had a daughter, Bessie and son Eric, who was to spend his working life as a tackler in the town's silk industry. Like us, later in the 30s they moved to Hurdsfield Estate and were our neighbours.

Taking a short cut up a ginnel by the side of the Co-op would bring us to Mrs Mullins' oatcake bakery. Her oatcakes, crumpets and scones were very highly regarded in the area. She had a son, Jack, a fine young man. A similar business to Mrs Mullins', and of equal standing, was conducted by the Simpsons in Fence Street which ran parallel to Waterloo Street. Their children, May, Eric and Kenneth enjoyed a close affinity to my brothers and sisters and remain good friends to this day.

Further down Fence Street there was another chippie. This was a garretted property kept by the Hodkinsons - son Derek would go to school with me in the early years - and lower down still, opposite the side of Daybrook Street School was Welch's little grocery and confectionery shop. They, too, usually had a nice range of cakes in the window. Other Fence Street names which come to mind are Worthington, Melvin, Blower, Gidman, Brierley, Jolliffe, Bradbury, Wooliscroft, Bloor, Wilkinson, Fray and Duffield.

Fence Street from Dickens Street corner where the Blower family resided for many years.
*Photo Macclesfield Express*

# Chapter Three
## My home

My home, 89 Waterloo Street, was exactly the same as all the other houses in that final stretch at the top left-hand side of the street; only the numbers of the houses were different. Two up, two down with a sash window to each room and a coal cellar beneath the kitchen at the back. The back door opened on to the Big Yard, as we called it, which stretched from the Victoria Park wall at the top, right down to behind the off-licence at the bottom where an entry led out into Dicken Street. The yard also served several Dicken Street houses as well.

Knock on any door on the street side of my row and it would open with the hinges on the left, and as the door opened, chances are there would be a large patch of Lincrusta on the wall just inside the door. It was common practice in those days to have such wall covering at this point, to protect what decor there was, since it was constantly being brushed against with clothing, and not only by the occupants. There were many 'club men' callers collecting their dues, usually on a Friday evening (wages night), and whatever the weather they would bring it in with them! Coal delivery men frequently found it necessary to lug their one hundredweight sacks through the house from front to back, to reach the cellar grid in the yard. This protective lincrusta patch was invariably painted with what was termed 'a serviceable colour', which usually meant dark brown!

The door of my home opened on to the side of an ornate mahogany sideboard of which I have only slight recollection. I do remember, though, that the left-hand side of the top drawer contained our assortment of club books, handy for speedy Friday evening presentation: Prudential, Provident Clothing, Penny Burial Society and others, about eight in total.

The table in the centre of the room had suspended above it a pulley clothes rack which was in constant use. Viewing the room with one's back to the sideboard, we had a singer sewing machine with a small coffin-like box atop on the left against the window, and against the right wall, a couch. Facing centre was the fire-grate, a black, regularly 'Zeboed' appliance bearing a plate declaring its Macclesfield origins and the name J H Cutts. It included an oven, a considerable boon to the family. The mantelpiece was graced with a pair of brass candlesticks (a wedding gift to my parents) and a clock placed dead centre. There was also a crucifix about eight inches high with a round jet black plinth and cross, and this religious influence was complemented by a framed reproduction of William Holman Hunt's 'The Light of the World' on the left side of the chimney breast which afforded a semblance of balance to the gas-bracket on the right.

Floor to ceiling built-in cupboards on each side of the fireplace completed the main furnishings of the room. The lower, smaller cupboard bottoms were sprinkled with Keating's powder to kill any creepy-crawlers. The small cupboard on the left contained the gas metre with a penny slot, a small collection of books and packs of bookmakers' cards. These latter belonged to my father and gave a clear indication where his main interest lay. When not employed in an 'orthodox' role he would often stand in as a bookies clerk and make a bob or two on the race course. We kids preferred him going to the Doncaster St Leger meeting for he would be sure to return with a supply of that town's celebrated butterscotch toffee.

The smaller cupboard on the right contained a heavy cobbler's last and an assortment of old boots and shoes. Why my parents were loath to dispense with old footwear is a question I am unable to answer; they must have believed that a potential, minimal as it was, remained. The big cupboard on the left housed our crockery - and we needed a fair amount of that - and the one on the right served as a pantry except for the top-most shelf which had a special function. A cardboard box hibernated on this shelf eleven and a half months of each year. It contained the most wonderful selection of glass Christmas tree decorations anyone could imagine. There were balls, lanterns, exotic birds with bushy tails, all of them multi-faceted and coloured, and generously embellished with gold and silver. I have seen nothing to compare with them since. Chairs in the room were placed where they could cause least hindrance between meals.

The floor was flagged and in my earliest days was uncovered and was scrubbed vigorously by my mother each week, her 'props' being a bucket of hot water containing a hand-scoop of Thom's soft soap, purchased from Norman's stall in the market-place, a scrubbing brush, a block of carbolic soap to produce a rich lather, and a floor-cloth for finishing. I hated this weekly upheaval and would make myself scarce for a while, returning to a home the front room floor of which was covered either with sheets of the Daily Dispatch or Sunday's News of the World, put down to ensure there was no contamination from dirty boots during the drying period.

The kitchen was, basically, a work place. We had a slopstone and a single water tap. A gas boiler, when not in use, acted as a stand for the gas

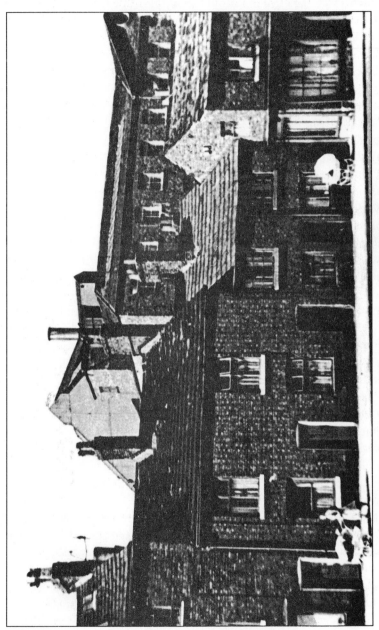

Commercial Road from the bottom of Waterloo Street. Thorpe Mill is in the background.

ring which, with the fire and the oven in the front room, comprised our home's total facilities for heating and cooking. A giant mangle stood close to the dividing wall, its two wooden rollers showing clear evidence of long service. In the middle roller area the wood was roughened and a slight gap had formed. Despite its size Mother turned the handle at the side with no great difficulty and regarded this monster as one of the best friends she had.

A large dolly-tub was strategically placed to catch the water when this operation took place. A dolly-peg posser played its part in the wash-day process. On the wall hung a zinc bath, a reminder of family-life ritual, and a small work table contributed a valuable utility role.

The chore of family washing (ours was Rinso assisted) was eased considerably by sending larger items, sheets for example, to the laundry each week. The name which springs to my mind at this point is 'Hyde and District Laundry', so the chances are that I am right, or why should I think of it? That Mother had a strict routine is confirmed by my remembrance of the price the laundry charged us each week, for the bill was always stuck on the outside of the brown paper parcel. It was two shillings and tenpence ha'penny, and worth every copper. True, on the odd occasion an item did get lost and it was irritating when it happened, but, in the main, I have to say this company's service was outstanding. Items sent had to have a laundry-mark sewn on them by the company and how they succeeded on such a scale in returning a complete list of items, impeccably laundered and pressed, week after week, with scarcely a hiccup, is beyond my comprehension. Needless to say, the odd loss was made good. Some shop, close to our home, must have acted as agency for the laundry. Mrs Clark's? Mrs Lancaster's? I really don't know.

The backs of our homes opened on to a flagged pavement but, that having been said, the Big Yard was a charmless dirt stretch with clumps of outside lavatories, two backing up against two, with a space for dustbins. These were built on the far side of the yard close to the wall dividing the Fence Street backs from our own. They were shared WC's. Two or perhaps three houses shared a particular one. Most were kept locked, for obvious reasons, and it was usual for each house's key to be threaded on strong string with a small cotton bobbin. These were hung behind back doors in readiness.....

Each lavatory had a small window and most inside surfaces had a thick crust of whitewash layers, the result of many annual applications. Families 'took turns' to clean them. All the backyard closets to which I had access in those days had sheets of rectangular pieces of newspaper, seven inches by five, threaded by string in one corner, hanging from a nail in the back of the door. I shudder to think of it now. It certainly gave another meaning to the term, 'the small print across the bottom'.

**A sketch by the author showing a pair of outside water closets, typical of Macclesfield in the 1930s**

The stretch of Fence Street where, in 1931, a young schoolgirl meeting a new boy pupil began a brief and poignant story. Daybrook Street Boys' School is seen on the corner.

## Chapter Four
## Starting school

I believe I was well prepared for school which I commenced in 1931 following my fourth birthday in June. With Eileen, Tony and Vincent already established on the educational path it was inevitable that some of their learning would rub off on me. The main influence came from Tony, a lad who found anything requiring deep thought in others of his age easy to do himself and a succession of teachers had recognised and applauded his brightness. He had a generous heart and was eager to offer encouragement to those less gifted than himself. I knew my alphabet and could recite it backwards as well. Actually, it had proved to be much easier to learn in reverse as it rhymed that way. I also had a basic understanding of numerals. I could tie my boot laces and had learned how to skip along the pavement, an accomplishment I rated very highly, but telling the time by the clock had still to be mastered.

On my first morning at Trinity Square School I was taken by Mother. This must have upset her routine for at that time she was employed by Tie Silks, Lower Heys, as a silk weaver on a 60 hours a week basis commencing at 6am each day. As I understand it she 'asked out' in order to return home at 8.30 to comply with what she considered a mother's duty on a child's first day at school.

I was handed over to young Miss Gibson, the first infant's class teacher. A Congleton lass, Miss Gibson arrived by train at Central Station each morning. Classes in those days were quite large and there were numerous other boys and girls experiencing the same uneasy baptism as me. We were shown the cloakroom and allocated the precise peg we were to use. We were then designated a desk and put at our ease by our charming teacher. A good looking young woman, Miss Gibson's skin had a golden glow, her natural colour, and I warmed to her right from the start. She was of average height, was neither thin nor bonny, and young though she was, she was a gifted teacher who prepared her wards with a grounding that was second to none. Indeed, this talented Miss commenced a sequence of quality teaching which embraced the union of Trinity Square and Daybrook Street Boys' School. Given also that she was kind and caring at all times it is no wonder I adored her and to my mind she was, like Baby Bear's porridge, chair and bed, Just Right!

29

Our first playtime is vivid in my memory. For a reason I have never understood we were not released into the playground by the short route from our own classroom, but were led, in jumbled formation, through the classrooms of the Misses Ingham and Mitchell to the main school corridor connecting front door to back. The narrowing of the back door caused a jam, all of us eager to relieve the claustrophobic feeling the apprehension of this first morning had induced. I was behind a little girl, more self-assured than the others, whose name was Nancy (I would learn the 'Hadfield' later). Trapped within a mass of small bodies I was content to be carried along by this living tide. In a small fruity voice Nancy chirped, "Don't these boys press so ...?" and at that I pressed all the harder!

Poignancy was to cloud my first few months at the school. On the morning of my second day at Trinity I set off, ostensibly to make the journey alone. I felt no trepidation, as the half mile walk entailed no traffic hazard. Early on, as I was walking down the centre of Fence Street, a little girl came from out of a doorway on the left and clasping my left hand in her right, said "I am taking you to school". Just like that. The act seemed to be so planned that I concluded that my mother must have arranged it. Margaret Duffield - for she it was - was a year or more older than I which made her something of a veteran in my eyes and I was perfectly happy to enjoy the company of this sweet girl. She delivered me to my cloakroom and continued in her role as chaperone for several weeks.

Then, abruptly, it all stopped. No longer was there an open door in Fence Street as I approached. No longer was there a Margaret coming without to clasp my hand. I asked Mother about it. Margaret was poorly, she said, and was not well enough for school.

At that point I became a trifle more adventurous on my school journey and would cut down Norton Street from Daybrook Street and walk through Gladstone Square. Once there I would often meet up with Gordon Plant whose parents had a fruit and vegetable shop - and fish too, perhaps - across the Square. However, Gordon's stay at Trinity was brief. The Plant's moved across town and Gordon continued his education at St Andrew's. In adult life he prospered in the haulage trade.

But what of that sweet little pal of mine? Time went by and the days got shorter and one night Mother returned from work with the news that Margaret was very poorly indeed. It was as if Mother preferred not to talk about it so the information was brief and ominous. Following tea that evening I made my way in the darkness to the pavement in Fence Street, opposite Margaret's home. Downstairs was all in darkness but a light was on in the bedroom above. I considered crossing the street and knocking and then reasoned that I would offend decency and probably disturb a critically ill child. I settled for a short, fervent prayer before returning home in an uncommunicative mood. The next day Mother said Margaret had 'gone to Jesus', and put that way, it did help, but I still feel her loss to this day.

There were many new names and faces in my life now and without exception they were a lovely bunch of chums: Ronald Sutton, Derek Wilson, Kenneth Haywood, Geoffrey Campsell, Roy Hall, Brian Surtees, Fred Slater, Philip Harding, Vernon Connor, Colin Smith, Derek Roberts, Stanley Kay, Roland Heywood, Geoffrey Pownall, Eric Lynch, Kenneth Stanway, Derek Hodkinson, Frank Gaskell, Bill Potts, Robin Wood, Geoffrey Sumner, Gerald Bradley and Stanley Macdonald.

The girls included Nancy Hadfield, Eileen Eaves, Fanny Nield, Sheila Craghill, Margaret Parr, Ellen Potts, Annie Fairbrother, the twins Joan and May Wheeldon, Irene Cunningham, Jean Curly, Ena Clarke and Patricia Lawton.

The playground at Trinity Square was like a walled plateau on one side overlooking folds of meadowland. I never knew the playground not to contain a huge pile of coke. Morning playtime was a special treat with the one-third pint bottle of fresh milk. The cream on top was nectar sipped through a straw via the hole in the cardboard disc on top. Boys playtime recreation seemed to be spent linking up, arms behind backs, in Tiller girl formation, singing out loudly, "Who'll join in for cowboys and Indians?" By the time sufficient lads had joined the line to justify battle it was too late to mime the firing of weapons or make explosive noises with the mouth.

It was not often that inclement weather denied us these pleasurable breaks but there was one morning of some significance when we were confined to our desks. My desk was directly in front of Miss Gibson's but was much lower than hers. Even so, I was able to discern everything that happened. Miss Gibson took from her desk a small package and carefully unwrapped it on her desk's level surface, spreading the paper out fully. She then raised a piece of fruit cake to her mouth and took a little bite, chewing this morsel daintily in the front of her mouth. Each successive bite was treated in like manner. It was a crumbly cake and with each bite a few crumbs of cake fell upon the wrapping paper. At last, when the solid body of cake had been consumed, Miss Gibson, with sliding movements of one hand, brought all the crumbs together to form a little pile in the centre of the

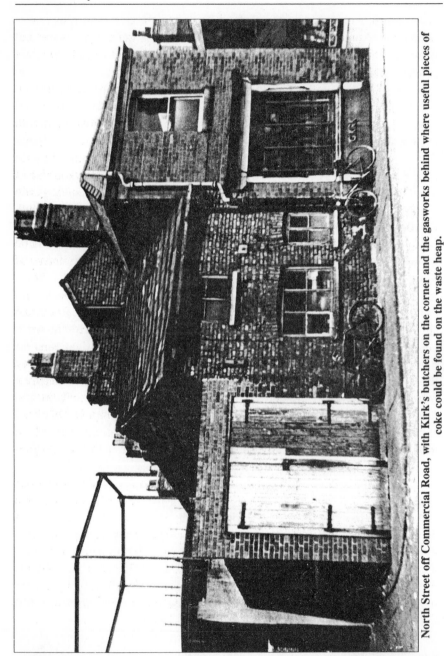

North Street off Commercial Road, with Kirk's butchers on the corner and the gasworks behind where useful pieces of coke could be found on the waste heap.

paper. Then, with a clawed hand, she descended on the mound squeezing it with a thumb and four fingers into a congealed pellet and popped it into her mouth. I was so impressed with all this I determined that I would enact this ceremony at home the first chance I got.

On a regular basis, Mother baked 'Cakeoma' in the roasting tin. Cakeoma was a product of Latham & Co. Ltd., Liverpool and London, and was advertised as 'The No-trouble Cake Maker'. A soft yellow pack with navy printing, it was bought from Mrs Clark's shop for sixpence. It is likely that for each baking Mother used two packs in order to fill the roasting tin and probably had to add an egg or two to work the magic. It would rise in the oven and bake to an appetising golden lustre, and when cooled would be cut into squares as needed. That very evening as tea-time neared its end, the roasting tin came out and Mother dexterously did her stuff with the knife. Ours was an oil-cloth covered table and I would have settled for that surface alone but, rather than draw attention to myself, my plate remained in place - a poor substitute for wrapping paper.

I took a little bite of my cake and tried chewing it in the front of my mouth as Miss Gibson had done but there seemed little joy in that and I shelved the idea almost immediately. A glance at my plate told me not a single crumb had fallen. I tried another little bite; again, the cohesive property of the cake denied me any pleasure. Rubbing the cake across my clenched teeth, surreptitiously, had limited success and in the end I sat there with both hands at my mouth, one holding the cake and the other breaking pieces off it and crumbling the cake between my fingers. I enjoyed the final act of bringing the crumbs together and lowering my hand on them like a crane's grab but, all things considered, it had been such a hassle, a repeat performance was never again considered.

Cake, it seems to me now, on reflection, was part of the ritual of our lives in those early days. On Friday evenings when Mother returned home from work we kids were each given a penny to go out and buy a cake from any shop of our choice to complement the evening meal. This explains why, in my narrative, I have made passing reference to cakes in shop windows. With my penny I would first visit and inspect Clark's, Pitcher's and Welch's windows at a run before investing my treasured coin. Following tea we would also be given a 'Friday's ha'penny'. A visit to Buxton Road and Crowder's shop was, for me, fairly automatic.

Waterloo Street. The Glazebrook family home has the milk on the window sill. Their entry (ginnel) led right back to where the Sherratt family's Dunbar Yard could be seen over the wall at the end of Davies Street.

## Chapter Five
## Spartan times?

It was a most pleasurable year, that first in Miss Gibson's class. So much of the work was practical. We had little pairs of scissors with rounded ends for shaping paper; crayons which had a most distinctive smell (purple was my favourite colour), plasticine, and sand trays as a writing and sketching medium.

One story book I remember well. Small in size, it was a hardback and quite advanced for a first reader. None of the words was 'fractured' to assist learning - a feature of Chick's Own comic, tuppence weekly - and stories were well illustrated with black and white drawings. One story was titled 'A Narrow Escape' and showed a cat running along the top of a wall in the moonlight. I considered that title probably the best in the whole world and vowed to use it myself some day.

Another story title I found puzzling (and no wonder), was 'Poor Wee Bairn'. It had a picture of a child sleeping in a babes-in-the-wood situation. Poor wee bairn? Fancy inflicting that on young Sassenachs so far south of the border. But we kids survived the puzzlement as we did later when informed that 'Mr' was Mister and 'Mrs' was Missus.

When school was finished each day and also at weekends I spent a good deal of my time in the Glazebrook's home across the street from us. Hubert was a wee bit older than me and went to St Paul's. He was more likely to be seen taking bites at a wedge of cheese, like a young Ben Gunn, than at a segment of, say, Madeira cake. Their home, number 58, like the rest of the houses on that side of the street, had a built-on scullery enabling them to 'live' in the middle room and retain the front room as a neat, tidy parlour, tastefully furnished with a piano for good measure. Hubert's father was a Northwich man with Welsh roots.

Daughter Annie, twelve or more years older than Hubert was something of a local celebrity, having been the Macclesfield Girls' Swimming Champion. She later married Harold Charlesworth and their first home was in Eastgate. But I digress. Mrs Glazebrook was a warm, gentle lady who had her elderly mother, Hubert's Granny Ratcliffe, living with them. In 1932, Granny was precisely eighty years old and it is interesting to note that when she was born in 1852, the daughter of a prosperous Macclesfield coal merchant, living literary 'giants' at that time included Charles Dickens, Elizabeth Gaskell, Charlotte Bronte, Alfred Tennyson, George Eliot, Alexandre Dumas and Harriet Beecher Stowe.

As was to be expected, Granny Ratcliffe spent much of her time sitting by the fire as it burned in the bungalow grate. On the day I write of Granny had just added coal to the fire and settled comfortably back into her chair when the air of tranquillity was interrupted by a loud explosion in the grate and missiles flew about the room. Poor Granny was hit in the left eye and the glass of a picture on the back wall was pierced as if by a small calibre bullet. The dear old lady was taken to Macclesfield Infirmary and detained, but, unfortunately, her eye could not be saved.

A full investigation showed the explosion had been caused by a small live mining detonator mixed in with the coal, and subsequently the local coal merchant who had supplied the coal (who could hardly be blamed for this shocking incident) offered Gran twenty pounds as compensation.

By this time there were eight of us Hunters in the cramped quarters of our two-up, two-down terraced house, plus our loyal retainer, Tum-tum the cat. The arrival of a final child, Terry, was to bring the family much joy following our return to the Hurdsfield Estate later in the decade.

The years I write of were difficult times for most folk. Dad still had problems finding sustained work but my mother's reputation as a talented and industrious silk weaver ensured her regular employment with Tie Silks, Lower Heys, working daily 6am to 6pm Monday to Friday and Saturday morning until 12 noon. The support given to us by Glegg Street nursery cannot be over-stated.

Often during the winter while Mother was in work, during Saturday mornings we children would take buckets and poking sticks to the Gas works waste heap at the junction of Thorp Street and North Street, off Commercial Road, and glean for useful pieces of coke for our fire. A metal bucket for this purpose and the stick for probing the ashes was essential since much of the coke was still hot! The light, silvery-coated coke was easy to spot even in the early light of dawn.

Today, I look back with pride at what my mother achieved. With limited resources available there was no place for frivolity in her caring nature. A superb cook, culinary marvels were produced as a matter of routine and in regard to finance, a 'bit' was put away each week to ensure that, come Barnaby, the family could have a week at Blackpool, albeit in modest circumstances. Fifty years on when Mother and I talked of the difficulties of those years she commented, "Geoff, I was never without a pound in my purse." A finer testimony to prudence I never heard.

The Barnaby holidays at Blackpool are worthy of reflection. We never, ever, booked for accommodation, probably with good reason for who can guarantee that all members of a large family will be enjoying good health on a specific future date? On the Friday evening two large suitcases were crammed with clothes and early on the morrow, with Dad in the role of pack-mule, we would join the exodus from either Hibel Road or Central Station. On arrival at the resort we made straight for the sands close to Central Pier and Mother and us kids would wait while Dad went in search of digs. Always, it seems to me, we stayed in Coop Street, off Chapel Street - the boarding houses are there to this day - about 150 yards from the pier. Mother would shop daily for our food and deliver it to our landlady for cooking; that was the approved cheap way of having a holiday at that time. A constant irritant to me was that a small ice cream cornet I could buy from a Granelli's cart at home for a ha'penny was double the price in Blackpool!

There was one year when during the holiday week my father had to go off for one of his racecourse duties as bookie's clerk. The meeting coincided with the retirement of a prominent jockey, and on the day, Dad played his hunch and backed every mount carrying this rider. Whether the jockey in question won all his races fairly or whether he owed anything to the generosity of his fellows is a matter for conjecture, but we Hunters were able to inhale good Irish Sea air for a further week!

A sparkle added to holiday life then was provided by the Daily Dispatch whose secret personality, Percy Pickles, would be advertised to appear in different resorts on specific dates. A cryptic photograph of him was published - perhaps the back of his head or his trilby hat concealing most of his face - and should a holidaymaker feel a confident sighting had been made, he (or she) was invited to challenge Percy, thus: "You are Percy Pickles; I read the Daily Dispatch regularly, and I claim the fiver." Needless to say, the Daily Dispatch was never benevolent towards us.

On reflection, it would be too severe to describe the early years of my family life as 'spartan'. Yes, we were poor but we had standards. Nothing but best butter or tasty dripping ever lubricated our bread. Our diet was wholesome and plentiful, albeit achieved by prudent purchase and preparation. We enjoyed good pea soup with a rich ham bone as foundation, potato pie fortified with meat from Mr Devonport's shop, and dumplings in our stew, for example, and we were regularly dosed with cod liver oil and malt.

Occasionally, if sniffles developed, we would be given a preparation of Norton's Oils and raspberry vinegar, and always in our cupboard were castor oil and syrup of figs, a panacea pairing Mother would not have been without. Medicines such as these were usually purchased from Mr Malin's chemist shop in Gladstone Square. A pleasing aspect of trading with Mr Malin at that time were the free gifts of 'burn-out' papers. With your purchase you would be given what appeared to be a plain sheet of white paper about eight inches by six. One side of the paper was marked with a spot. Once back home the paper would be placed on a plate in the centre of the table, spot side uppermost, and all of us would crowd round. The end of a piece of string would be lighted, blown out, and the glowing end made to touch the spot on the paper. The effect was as if a fuse had been lit (which, in fact, it had) and a slow burning trail - an invisible salt petre printed line - would eventually portray an animal or bird. These sheet entertainments were good fun and very safe when adult-supervised.

In the winter, on particularly cold nights, a hot oven shelf, wrapped in brown paper, would be placed in each of our beds (three of us in each bed). Prayers were said nightly and were in three parts; a prayer for safety during the night, the Lord's prayer, and a prayer of thanks, ending with a list of God-blesses. Chamber pots were a necessity given our circumstances, as they were in most other homes then. Train noises were always for me a comforting sound at night. The railway and its accompanying sidings beyond Commercial Road found a ready auditory canal in Waterloo Street, and the sound of shunting, clanging buffers and the rhythmic metallic stutter of speeding trains, their whistles screaming through the night, carried readily up the full length of the street and was a soothing reminder of the friendly monsters, eager to do our bidding. Like many other enthusiasts, I retain a great affection for the muck and the majesty of steam locomotion.

I am not alone, I know, in linking past times to music and song, but oddly enough, the earliest songs I recall were not contemporary compositions at all - consider the songs 'Daisy, Daisy' and 'In the shade of an old apple tree', and a special favourite of mine (and of HRH Princess Margaret also), 'If you were the only girl in the world'. These were golden oldies even in those days.

Rhyme played a part in our lives as well. Kids new to our area had to be alert when accosted thus:

Adam and Eve and Pinch-me-Well
Went down to the sea to bathe;
Adam and Eve were drowned,
Who d'you think was saved?

Among many other things, these were the days of the Bisto kids on the hoardings and the sporting weekly, Topical Times; of the Rainbow, Tiger Tim's Weekly, Playbox and Sunbeam comics, retailing at tuppence and their poorer relations, Comic Cuts, Chips and Jingles at a penny; of the itinerant street singer and ginger beer in earthenware jars; of 'pobs', and gas mantles with their three splayed feet and chain-cases on bicycles; string in abundance which Co-op counter-hands could snap with their fingers with more ease than most others could break cotton thread, smoothing irons with 'shoes', John Bull printing outfits, Colman's mustard in small oval tins, brown paper carrier bags with string handles, Charlie from Rainow and, peculiar to Macclesfield, Cook's Ices.

This last will puzzle a few, I bet. Cook's ices were dispensed from white hand-pushed boxes which trundled along painfully on wheels far too small for our street surface. I never did taste Cook's ices; Mother was too set in her Granelli ways to consider any alternative other than the pedal-powered Wall's 'Stop me and buy one' cart. Wall's seemed to sell just two items in those days. Tuppenny wrapped bricks of pure white ice-cream - a novelty of those times usually eaten from out of the paper wrapper - and penny fruit ices. These 'Snow Fruits' were three-sided packets (Toblerone shape), open at each end, with a small dark-blue chess board design and filled with frozen fruit juice. They were the fore-runners for our traditional ice lollies. When first purchased, the trick was to roll the pack vigorously between the palms of both hands to loosen the contents. The ice could then be slid upwards from the bottom for sucking convenience and the bottom wrapping curled tooth-paste-tube fashion to contain the melting juice.

But to return to Cook's Ices, I am informed by Mr Morris Cliffe of Macclesfield that Cook's premises were in Catherine Street, having previously belonged to Granelli's, not the Granelli's of longstanding Macclesfield repute, but another family from the Parma area of Northern Italy, where it is a common family name.

The station and sidings at Hibel Road, from which comforting sounds emanated throughout every night.

## Chapter Six
## Growing up

Following my fifth birthday in 1932 it was with some regret that I left Miss Gibson's class at Trinity and moved up to Miss Mitchell's class, Standard 2. The term 'moved up' is deliberately chosen here for although Miss Mitchell's class was on the same floor and the move was on a horizontal plane, there was always a sense of accomplishment when one achieved a numerical rise in class standards and this sense of elevation did tend to soften the blow of bidding Miss Gibson adieu.

Miss Mitchell was a kindly lady with long experience of teaching. She lived at Forest Cottage on the Macclesfield/Buxton road. I believe she shared her home with Miss Ingham, the teacher of Standard 3. Religious instruction was very marked in Miss Mitchell's class, with an early morning period of prayer and chanting each day before getting down to normal lessons.

My new classroom contained a large glass case of stuffed birds, and when the occasion warranted it, a maypole which could be slotted into a hole in the floor. I did not take too kindly to the mawkish ritual of holding on to a strand of ribbon and wending my way, in and out with other pupils, and moving round and round weaving plaited patterns on the wooden pole.

I fell in love with a beautifully tuned song which began, *"Come little leaves", said the wind one day, "Come o'er the meadows with me and play ..."* Another clever little number was 'Mr Nobody'. Mr Nobody, it seemed, was the funny little man in everybody's house who would never admit to being the culprit of mis-doings. I recognised then that this song was very true-to-life for we had a Mr Nobody in our house!

In the winter we had hot Horlicks in nursery rhyme beakers, and one morning I was given a McVitie & Price plain chocolate digestive biscuit. It seems ridiculous now, more than sixty years later, that I should recall the gift of a single biscuit, but the rippled chocolate on the surface was so thick the pleasure of that treat has never been forgotten. A rhyme we were taught in those days etched itself, indelibly, on my mind as well.

> "Let us to bed", says Sleepy Head.
> "Let's stay awhile", says Slow;
> "Put on the pan", says Greedy Nan,

"We'll sup before we go!"

Cleverness, such as that, helped to stimulate in me a literary awakening.

My route going to Trinity was always up Hurdsfield Road to Bamford Street then cutting through to Lansdowne Street and the school. Going home, though, was invariably down the length of Lansdowne Street, picking my way carefully, since the surface was rough. As I write of the street now I am reminded of the joyous scent of fresh ripening apples from the allotments on the left. Apples then, were not the common treat they are today and if a lad was spotted eating one there would soon be a plea of "Will you save us (me) your core?", and once a pledge had been made he would be reminded to "Leave us some on!" once his teeth had completed a full circuit of the fruit.

There was a period when I arrived home first from school and had to climb up to the window and raise it slightly to get the front door key. There was a foot-hold of sorts but it wasn't easy and it was less easy on the day a bitter blizzard was raging and my feet and hands were numb. I honestly felt I was close to death that day but somehow managed to get into the house but failed to get the fire to kindle. I curled up into a ball on the sofa to await the arrival of the others. All was well in the end but not before I suffered the most painful agony in toes and fingers as circulation was restored.

There was also a time when it was arranged for a Mrs Norbury to be on hand at home after school to make jam butties and drinks for us. I knew of no link connecting this Mrs Norbury with the family of that name at number 77, nor, so far as I could judge, did she live in the vicinity, so this lady remains something of a mystery to me to this day. Excellent woman she may have been but I had one tacit criticism of Mrs N. As she dexterously applied liberal butter to bread she would catch the knife on the edges of the bread slices and the result was that each folded sandwich had butter protruding beyond its boundary. I hated this and would rub the edge of each butty vigorously with a finger to massage the butter into invisibility.

At times I would stand on the flags in the yard listening to Mother updating old Mrs Rose, our next door neighbour, with local gossip. In the earliest days I was puzzled by the old lady's seemingly offensive attitude to my mother when a tasty morsel of tattle had been imparted. Mrs Rose would wave an admonishing hand at Mother and exclaim, "Get away wi' yer!" or "Gerr-o-o-o-off!" but my mother would carry on talking, quite unconcerned.

Those backyard flags were too uneven for childrens' games and

Trinity Square School 'siblings' 1932-33

Back row: Kenneth Arnold, Ivan Heywood, Philip Johnson, Vincent Hunter, Geoffrey Pownall, Mary Pownall, Raymond Bradley.
2nd row: Gerald Barber, Roland Heywood, Douglas Johnson, Gerald Bradley, Geoffrey Hunter, Nora Smith.
3rd row: Audrey Frith, Mary Houghton, Neville Wilson, Derek Wilson, Jessie Houghton, Catherine Arnold, Winifred Barber.
Front row: Olwen Potts, Ellen Potts, Bernard Frith, Colin Smith.

hopscotch and skipping sessions were enjoyed - mainly by the girls - on the street's front flags. Small kitchen tiles were often used for hopscotch and skipping ropes were commonplace. I loved to hear the songs the girls chanted as the rope went round and round and feet danced daintily on the stone surface. It might be Renee Norbury and Mary Parton at each rope-end doing the twirling and singing and Ivy Sherratt bobbing between the two. One of the songs went, "There's somebody under the bed, whoever can it be ...?" Since I lived in constant fear of someone being under my bed I listened attentively to this song in the hope of learning the rascal's identity, but I never did.

Recreation for us youngsters had to be obtained at very little cost, if any at all. Victoria Park was a boon. It was, and still is, like a proud cottage. The 'bottom park', as it was called, where we played most of our games, could be likened to a living room. This was before the days the roundabout type of equipment was installed but we did have two areas of swings, one on the Fence Street side of the park and the other on the Daybrook Street/Fence Avenue corner where the park lodge was situated and housed Mr Blakelow, the park-keeper, and his wife.

The top park with its bandstand, bowling green, flower beds, trees and neatly manicured borders complemented with scalloped edges of thick steel wire, could be likened to a parlour - the best room. Another feature throughout the park were huge craggy pieces of granite used to edge the paths in special areas. Mr Roscoe, his wife and son Roger occupied the lodge here. Later in that decade they would move to lower Brocklehurst Avenue. Concerts in the bandstand were fairly frequent in the summer months, mid-week and weekends, and were welcome and sedate events. Trestle money-boxes were placed on these occasions at points of entry to the top park and the contributions were gratefully accepted by the incumbent musicians.

The park was enclosed by either high walls or substantial railings around its perimeter and the two main gates at Buxton Road and Daybrook Street and the Puzzle-gate in Fence Avenue were opened and locked at varying times each morning and evening throughout the year depending on the daylight hours. The park was not impregnable during the closed hours but in my experience the rules of entry were respected as a matter of course.

I was hanging around the top of Waterloo Street one day kicking my heels and wishing that Lonsdale & Adshead's lorry would arrive with a delivery for the Inn. That was always a spectacle worth watching as the two pavement doors were unfolded and crates of Guinness, pale ale, nut brown and other licensed victuals were slid down the ramp and hogsheads of beer were lowered into the cellar with restraining ropes. Then I heard the call, "Sonny!".

Miss Smith was at her door at the top house beckoning me with a coaxing finger and a benign smile. Such a pose was out of character for Miss Smith; usually she was irate (but never profane) and insistent that my group take our play elsewhere. Nor, come to think of it, could she be blamed, for her house, being the end one at the top, had its gable-end flanking the dirt patch leading to the Big Yard. The side of her house was convenient for ball games - football 'shooting in', cricket or just plain bouncing and catching. At times the poor woman must have thought her home was haunted by a phantom percussionist. A thin, plain woman, in her late thirties at the time, I would guess, she always seemed to be in residence.

The call to me, then, was a change of tune and I approached her curiously. "Do you know where the post-box is on Buxton Road?", she asked. I answered yes to that and a hand came from behind her back holding a letter. "Would you be good enough to post this for me, quickly?" As I nodded and accepted the letter the back of the letter was uppermost, and sensing there was some significance in this, I lowered the letter to my side as a gesture of indifference and turned to do her bidding. "Wait," she said. "When you have posted it I want you to come back here. All right?" I nodded my assent, my mercenary instincts now aroused by her command. I sped off along York Street, making for the post-box set in the wall directly opposite the Alms houses.

Halfway along the street, still holding the letter low, I slowed down and glanced behind me. Miss Smith had left her doorway and walked the few extra feet up the street in order to follow my progress. Noting this pause in my mission she crouched low and with both arms and hands shooed me to increase my tempo, and within moments I was round the corner into Buxton Road and out of her sight. I think it likely that I looked at the face of the letter at that point but as a defiant gesture only and with total disinterest. Having posted it I enjoyed the luxury of contemplation and expectation. Would my reward be a very useful ha'penny, or an apple or orange? A chocolate biscuit I would long remember? Miss Smith was in view throughout my return along York Street and only returned to her doorway as I crossed the street from the pub.

"Is the letter posted?"

**Give a dog a cone! This charming picture, about 1932, supplied by Granelli Ices, shows one of their salesmen Leo Costello in Arbourhay Street with the Elephant and Castle public house inthe background. The style of the cart had remained unchanged since the beginning of the century. The pail at the front contained a little water and the metal wafer-sandwich maker.**

"Yes."

"Can you remember to whom the letter was addressed?"

I shook my head slowly in response to that leading question, endeavouring to create an air of incomprehension.

"Surely you can remember the name on the letter?"

In a calculated bid to end this interrogation and reach the reward stage, I replied, "I never looked at the letter."

She smiled happily at that - and promptly shut her door, leaving me disconsolate on the flags!

When Mother came home from work I told her of my disappointment. "He that expecteth never receiveth," quoth she, unsympathetically.

It was rare for school children to misbehave seriously in my day and rarer still for me to witness any misdemeanour, which doubtless explains why the memory of an incident has stayed with me through the years. Returning from school along Daybrook Street one afternoon I spotted Mr Harold Rose, the Granelli ice cream salesman trundling his handcart towards me having already passed the school. As he reached the top of Norton Street on the park side, he left his cart by the kerb, crossed the street and vanished down an entry to pay a quick call to his home. No sooner had he disappeared than the Class 5 boys from upstairs at Daybrook spilled out of the school. One big lad spotted the ice cream cart immediately and shouted to four or five of his cronies to follow him. Quickly the lid was removed from the ice cream container and one after another, these lads - none of whom I knew - reached in and scooped huge dollops of the stuff before running back and up Fence Street with their spoils.

I was sickened by this disgusting theft and recognised the wrong being done. Today, I lament that youngsters twice the age I then was are reckoned to be below the age of responsibility and cannot be prosecuted. Makes you think, doesn't it?

This photograph, contributed by Mrs Abigail Robertson of Dundee, shows her Uncle Bill Garlick (wearing cap) who was for many years the highly respected supervisor at the New Cinema, Buxton Road, and her brother Jack Cobham with his wife Alice and young Barbara, enjoying the delights of Braemar.

## Chapter Seven
## The cinema

Try as I may I cannot recall the very first time I attended the Cinema picture house at the bottom of Buxton Road. I can date it though, fairly accurately, and I have always considered myself extremely lucky and privileged, that in a century severely scarred by war in its teenage years and having entered, falteringly, into its twenties, it could, by the time of my birth in 1927, have evolved a mode of entertainment which was to provide a rich golden seam of pleasure throughout my life; to wit, talking pictures. I reckon therefore, that it must have been during 1930 that I accompanied my sister Eileen, the eldest, and brothers Tony and Vincent from our home in Waterloo Street to my first Saturday matinee at that theatre. Leslie and Dorothy were to make the same short pilgrimage from the same house in their turn and our youngest brother, Terry, not born until the late thirties, would continue the family's patronage well into the forties.

Each Saturday, clutching our tuppences, we would troop down Eastgate at about 2pm. The first part, on the left, was taken up by Fence Sunday School and on the right, the back of Booth's bakehouse, followed by the Boundary Tavern. Across the street from the pub lived the Hodkinsons and the Osbornes. Both sizeable families, Wallace and Gordon of the former and Charlie of the latter were known to me at that time. A right-angled turn would lead us into King Street passing the Turner boys' home on the left. A left turn there and it was but a few short steps to Buxton Road with Billington's newsagents on the left corner, Perkin's sweet shop on the right corner followed by the Cinema itself.

Across the road was the formidable Old Royal Oak public house with its familiar model of an oak tree in full foliage contained in a glass case over the front door. This was on the corner of Davenport Street and if one cared to walk some distance up the street's gentle gradient to a point close to the Public Baths and view the theatre from that elevated position, the full title of New Cinema could be seen in white paint on its roof. Not that it was so new. It had been built and functioned as a cinema since 1912.

Throughout my Saturday matinee years between 1930 and 1938 and from then until 1945 as a regular patron (at which point King George VI sought to strengthen his Army with my presence) the Cinema staff would seem to have been a pretty durable bunch for they remained in attendance throughout. Mr Ernest Mellor was manager and his son Arthur was projectionist. Miss Savage - who lived in the middle one of three cottages between the bottom of the theatre slope and the Town's Yard - was in the pay-box, and Mr Garlick, from around the corner in Eastgate, was employed in a utility role. An ex-Sergeant-Major, firm and fair, he ensured that law and order prevailed off the screen as well as on! Occasionally before performances, he would move up and down the aisles spraying disinfectant from a Flit-type can.

Having been built well back from the road, the Cinema had a broad expanse of flagged pavement in front of it, so necessary for the queuing public. Since this area also incorporated Perkin's sweet shop premises, several yards of railings separated the two businesses, giving each an aspect of independence. Although Perkin's was ideally placed for trade it was not a shop which attracted me. To borrow a modern term it tended to be a wee bit 'up market' for my taste and was not a 'ha'penny place' in my eyes, a halfpenny being the maximum currency available to me for sweets at any one time. In passing, it may be of interest to reflect, for the benefit of readers far younger than myself, that in the days I am describing there were 480 halfpence to the pound.

Miss Savage's box-office faced directly on to the flagged forecourt, and the theatre's facia, in common with most others at that time, had two large glass-covered display cases containing, in one, photo-stills of the current evening main-feature film, and in the other, stills of the next main attraction. Having purchased their tickets, patrons entered the foyer through a door to the right. Once inside, doors to the toilets were on the right - the gents was kept well cleaned but oh, it was so pokey - with the main door to the auditorium on the left. This doorway was placed directly above the left gangway which separated the short row of seats by the left wall from the main seating area in the centre. This arrangement was mirrored on the right with a further gangway and wall seating. However, the theatre lost marks for symmetry here for this gangway and wall seating went further back than the rest into an odd little alcove which, it has to be said, at evening performances attracted couples more interested in each other than in the visual and audible bill of fare!

Two crash doors in the left wall, one halfway down and the other at the bottom, each with a gas-lit exit sign above, were used to good effect after each performance to facilitate speedy egress.

My earliest memories of the Cinema are the ones I cherish above all.

In those days the theatre had a lottery scheme at these Saturday matinee performances whereby the halves of tickets retained by the usherettes were placed in a box and shuffled just in front of the stage by Mr Garlick before the show commenced. One half ticket was drawn each week and following his loud disclosure of the magical number several hundred kids would check their halves in hopes of a match and the prize. This particular week Eileen, having confirmed that my half ticket matched, urged me to take it to the front and claim my prize. This down-hill walk was to the accompaniment of good-natured cheers and whistles from the losers.

Mr Garlick, having perused my portion of ticket and confirmed that justice was being done, reached into his right coat pocket and brought forth a sparkling silver torch or 'flashlight' as we called them in those days, complete with battery and all ready to light up my life! These retailed at the enormous sum of sixpence and, by my family's standards, this prize was equivalent to a birthday gift from my parents.

But now I come to the interesting part of the story. It was with good reason that Eileen had insisted that I present my half ticket personally to Mr Garlick. Some weeks previously when she had checked and found my brother Vincent's ticket to be a winner she had left him in his seat and approached Mr Garlick on his behalf. On that occasion Mr G had reached into his *left* coat pocket for the prize. When Eileen returned to her seat and handed Vincent his award he was disgusted to receive a string of beads! We can all smile at that incident now.

A further interesting incident occurred a month or so later by which time the lottery idea had been dropped by the management. Having arrived at the theatre later than usual, my family group ended up separated in the front stalls. I found myself seated next to a lad, a stranger to me, who appeared to be about six years old - two years my senior.

His first comments and actions made a most illuminating point. He explained that by smoothing down the red velvet on the back-rest of the seat with the palm of a hand one could then draw pictures on the velvet with the tip of a finger provided the sketching finger moved in an upwards direction at all times. Even a finger moving sideways and only slightly upwards achieved a sufficient ruffling of the velvet pile to produce a line on the smooth surface. With the few minutes of light available to us before the show commenced we engaged in artistic competition and then this bright little chap evidently reminded himself that he could educate me further.

"When you come 'ere," he said, "always make sure that your seat is not broke. Cos if you're caught in a broke seat they lock you up, up there." He pointed his artist's finger in the general direction of the back of the theatre.

To my query of "Up where?", he replied: "See them black 'oles up there? Well, if they catch you in a broke seat you get locked up behind 'em!"

At my impressionable age this seemed to be a perfectly feasible story since I - and he, for that matter, it would seem - knew nothing of film projection and the need for apertures in the back walls of cinemas. He increased my sense of unease, just as the theatre's lights were dimming to commence the show, by actually disclosing the names of two boys who were, at that very moment, incarcerated in that high dungeon.

I never saw that lad again after that memorable afternoon but I made jolly sure that each week from that point on the seat I chose was, so far as I could judge, in a good state of health. His sketching tip, though, was to serve me well for years. Hitherto, there had been nothing to fill the void awaiting the start of the show other than a repetitive sequence of orchestral offerings. Such sounds may have bored me then but that is not the case today.

The balance of programme remained unchanged throughout the years. There would be a short feature to start with - MGM's Our Gang with their cast of child actors were great favourites. Popular comedian Andy Clyde might oblige or another of that ilk, Edgar Kennedy. Chaplin silents too, retained a welcome link with the past, and who remembers the Bouncing Ball singing series? The words of songs in syllabic form would be displayed in white lettering on the screen, the music would play and a small white ball would appear bouncing rhythmically and precisely on each syllable as it moved along each line. These were the only occasions when Mr Garlick encouraged noise! A popular number of this genre at the time went: "When the red, red, rob-in, comes bob, bob, bobb-in, a-long, a-long ..."

Following this bit of excitement there would be a newsreel; Paramount, I think, borrowed from the evening programme, and then would come the main feature film. These films were mainly low-budget Westerns starring popular cowboy heroes of the time. Tom Mix with his horse 'Tony', Buck Jones, Tim McCoy and Ken Maynard. The latter with his horse 'Tarzan' was my favourite mainly because of his ability to withstand the rigors of the wildest western life and any amount of trail-dust, and yet still retain an immaculate image. Another US favourite we enjoyed seeing was the wonder dog Rin Tin Tin who showed far more intelligence than most of the humans in his films.

But American film-makers were not allowed to rule the roost entirely. British films featuring comedian Leslie Fuller and others, proved to be an acceptable diet.

The programme always concluded with a cliff-hanging serial episode calculated to bring the customers back a week later. The hero or heroine would be facing certain death at the end of the episode, to survive in miraculous fashion in the next, but the outrageous dishonesty of film-serial makers was totally acceptable to the audience since the formula maintained suspense between instalments. Serials I recall from my earliest Cinema days are 'The Mystery Man', who had an amphibious craft, 'The Lost Special', the story of a locomotive which vanished into thin air on a journey from A to B. How a story-line as thin as that was made to last for twelve or more episodes I cannot remember, which is, perhaps, just as well. And then we had 'The Masked Rider' a western. Following the first episode I informed my chums confidently "It's the girl!" This notable piece of perception came to me from my brother Tony, and sure enough, in the final episode, when the mask and the hat were snatched from the masked rider's head, her dark tresses cascaded defiantly about her shoulders. I enjoyed that.

But the serial that gets my vote from those days depicted US detective Craig Kennedy in 'The Clutching Hand'. Now there was a theme worthy of longevity. No need to describe what happened in that one! Golden days, indeed. Thank you, Mellor family and staff, and thank you, Silver Screen.

Arbourhay Street, looking down towards the Waterloo Street area taken from Brocklehurst Whiston's Mill.

## Chapter Eight
## Childhood friends

Sundays - mornings in particular - were quite demanding for Mother. At 12 noon the previous day she had completed a 60 hour week at Tie Silks, but there was no stinting in her effort to provide her family with the most comprehensive repast, come 1pm on the Sabbath. A traditional roast dinner, substantially served, with a sweet to follow, was prepared as wash-day got under way. Mother had a 'system' and demands made upon Dad were minimal. Always, though, there was a leisurely start to the day. Each week one of our brood would get up early and prepare and serve tea and biscuits to those in bed. There was a rota to this duty and no time was lost in teaching a younger member this early morning task.

It is an indication of how young I was when conscripted that on the morning of my initiation I had no idea that measures of coarse, dark brown dust had to be put into the pot before adding boiling water. Our large, dark brown tea-pot, I learned, needed more than its own colour to produce what was desired!

Later, following a bacon butty breakfast (with bread dipped in the 'dip') we kids were instructed to make ourselves scarce. Sometimes Dad would take us for a walk - Barracks Lane and Swan's Pool beckoned strongly on these occasions - but, more frequently, two or three of us would be encouraged by Mother to visit our maternal grandmother, Granny Talbot, who lived at 28, Arbourhay Street. Even in those distant times, Granny was in her mid-sixties and had three young men (our uncles) to take care of.

The route we took was always via Dicken Street and Fence Street where most of our friends lived. A grand bunch of pals they were too; I think warmly of them to this day. Undoubtedly, there was so much consideration for each other then, and once friends, you were bonded for life. Early in Dicken Street there was the Baker family who lived directly opposite the Big Yard entry. Frank was the eldest of the children; a tall, handsome lad, he had sisters Barbara, Gladys, Doris, and at a later date, Mary. I cannot think of Frank today without thinking also of Sinnett's, Fruit and Vegetable Merchants, Adelaide Street, for whom he drove for many years.

Across from them were the Rowleys with son Gordon and daughter Elsie. Many years later Gordon was to achieve fame as a mature student at

Cambridge University studying archaeology and gaining a Master of Arts degree. Mr Rowley once responded to an SOS from my mother when my younger brother, Leslie's leg was burned having been 'caught' by a hot shovel. Mr Rowley called daily for a period of time and did a magnificent job and Mother never forgot it; fifty years on she was still singing Mr Rowley's praises! It would appear from this story that this caring gentleman was in the Ambulance Service or something similar.

Still in Dicken Street, Roy Dickens was to remain a valued friend throughout his life. His father worked on the dustbins and on one occasion found the body of a new-born baby, wrapped in newspaper. It was sensational at the time, as was to be expected. Close by the Dickens lived Kathleen Kay and Jessica Dutton and opposite, little Peggy Slater. At the last house on the left before Fence Street, resided the Wards, Arthur and his sisters, Florence being the eldest, though Mary and Muriel were best known to us. The final stretch of Dicken Street beyond Fence Street, as it ended at the park railings, contained the home of Peggy and Winifred Bracegirdle.

As I picture the intersection of these two streets a whole new set of faces emerge to generate additional inner-warmth. In the upper part of Fence Street lived the Simpsons, May, Eric and Kenneth who I have previously referred to, and Harry Newton, Jack Wilkinson, Geoffrey Worthington and Sandy Melvin were also thereabouts, and on the lower corner of this junction, on the far side, lived the Blowers. There was Harry, Philip, Albert and other young ones. Harry, who answered happily to his nickname 'Mick', laughed more than anyone I have ever known, no matter how life's dice fell. Indomitable is the word, I believe.

Back on the other side again, I well remember Philip Brierley passing the exam for the Central School and seeing him bedecked in his new green jacket, cap and tie, with the yellow trimmings. Derek Davenport and sister Marion came shortly afterwards. A scout par excellence throughout the years since, Derek has earned a salute from us all. And then there was Jack Wooliscroft who shone so brightly at school, and Joe Fray and Bob Leach, and the darling child, Margaret Duffield, whose early passing has already been recorded, and Derek Hodkinson, in whose attic above the chip-shop we enjoyed uninhibited play at that time.

Just around the corner in Daybrook Street lived young Brian Bushell and his father, Percy, who was as young in heart as his son, and the Goslings of whom Kenneth was as tough as teak. Others on the Daybrook level were tall Jack Edwards, Len Wadkins (or Watkins) and young Jimmy Kirkham whose home faced the beginning of the park railings after the school playground wall ended.

Down to the Fence Tavern and the turn into Arbourhay Street would bring us to a cluster of long-established families whose children were all senior to me. The names of the Houghton children were known to me, since they were my mother's cousins - their father, Edmund, had been Granny Talbot's youngest brother. They were Ethel, Tom, Jack, Marion, Arthur, Herbert and Neville. Alongside them lived the Sherratts with five children, and up an entry in 1 court, 2 house, were the Tomkinsons. Their seven children included Ronald who, sixty and more years on, retains an abundance of memories of those times. Across the street, near to Miss Pimblott's shop, lived the Stubbs family, four children, and a few yards on, on the tavern side again, the Garforths at the Beaconsfield Club, with son Stanley; and closer to Norton Street, the Pownalls with the largest family of all, ten children. Bill and Les Jessop were somewhere thereabouts and in lower Norton Street were the Brooks family with Philip and Raymond and on the bottom corner, Taylor's butcher's boasted son Geoff, an outstanding swimmer, his brother Stanley and sister Marjorie.

We never stayed very long at Granny Talbot's. We would answer her questions about school, report on family health and any minor happening worth mentioning, then Granny (who had plenty of her own jobs to do) would say: "Call at Miss Pimblott's and ask her to give you a quarter of caramels between you." Now, Miss Pimblott - 'Polly', as she was commonly called - kept a house-cum-shop at the Fence Street end of Arbourhay, opposite the Tavern. There was nothing to indicate that hers was anything other than an ordinary house. Her door was usually ajar, and as a couple of us stepped inside onto the mat, Miss Pimblott, tasselled shawl about her shoulders, would rise from her fireside chair to attend to our needs. Two or three bottles of sweets in view seemed to indicate her entire stock. Just what else constituted a shop, apart from the snuff she supplied, I cannot think. We would repeat Granny's instruction and the bag of caramels would be handed over without any exchange of money, there being 'an understanding' between the two ladies. Sorry to relate, there was always a sting in the tail. Miss Pimblott's caramels, which normally weighed in at twenty sweets to the quarter, were long past their sell-by date - had one existed - and softened to fudge by the passing of time. Oh, yes, we ate them, complaining only to ourselves, but it did seem such a waste of Granny's money when at the time there was such a rich assortment elsewhere.

This unsatisfactory situation was changed in due course when Miss Pimblott carried a new line, recommended by Granny - 'mystery bags' at a ha'penny each. Once one or two had been bought they weren't such a mystery at all. Each bag contained some pop-corn, a few sweets, a small tin toy (whistle or clicking frog) and an item we used to call 'locust bean'. Strictly speaking, I believe the term should have been 'locust pod'. Locust pods, which I have not seen for donkey's years, were hard, dark brown, flattened dried pods, five or six inches long and were the product of a Mediterranean tree. One needed to nibble the strong brittle pods with care in order to avoid eating the small brown seeds they contained. The taste was of strong sweet tea. Now and again in our careful search for seeds, we would come across a maggot and would break off the contaminated area with a thumb-nail before continuing the nibbling. Definitely not a snack to take to the pictures!

A good brand of caramels on sale at that time at tuppence per quarter (no shop hesitated to sell you one ounce) was Sovereign, King of all Toffees. Other similar priced sweets were aniseed balls, mint imperials, liquorice torpedoes and a variety of liquorice novelties, including liquorice root; ju-jubes (small fruit pastilles), Maynard's wine gums, gob stoppers, bars of Roocroft's nougat, ribbed sticks of coltsfoot rock, pink and white coconut chips and coconut ice and a fondant mixture described as 'Ducks, new potatoes and green peas'.

Popular chocolate manufacturers of the day were Cadbury - they made ha'penny bars - Rowntree, Fry, Caley (makers of the first Crunchie bars), Nestle and Mars. Packer's of Bristol failed dismally to win any support from me. Their chocolate drops I would not even accept as a gift after the first tasting.

In addition, a wide range of boiled sweets included perennials, humbugs, acid and pear drops. And there was chewing gum - which leads me right in to an interesting little story.

# Chapter Nine
## School, chewing gum and cats cradle

When first invited to sample chewing gum, which was sold in four small sugared tablets per packet for a ha'penny and six larger tablets for a penny, I was warned of the consequences of swallowing the pliable substance. "It will swell in your belly and kill you," I was told. I forget which lad actually told me this but I'm certain he did so in good faith as two other boys present nodded sagely.

I was aged about five at the time and, naturally, the prospect of dicing with death simply to appear American was something that had to be considered seriously.

In the end, confidence in numbers and infallible belief in the control I had over my throat muscles won the vote and I accepted the first of many white tablets (there was no strip gum in those days), and for the next 12 months I masticated - tentatively at first, then joyously, with impunity. Then one day Mother said, "Geoffrey, I think you're big enough now to go to Livesey's for the chips," and I was handed the big basin and sixpence, told to watch out for the traffic on Buxton Road, and off I went. I was chewing gum at the time .....

Livesey's chip-shop was almost directly opposite the Dunbar opening and the chip transaction went smoothly. I came away from the shop with my basin full and well insulated with clean tissue paper and a generous covering of newspaper. Returning back through the Dunbar I reasoned that I had earned a taste of chip and, clasping the basin firmly to my solar plexus with my left hand and arm, I wriggled my right hand inside the newspaper and up the side of the basin, hurriedly withdrawing a long hot chip and placing it rapidly on the newspaper cover where I could blow and cool it. It was then I remembered my chewing gum. I reckoned, on reflection, that I had become so proficient in the art of chewing that I could confidently relegate the gum to a 'no danger' area in the right side of my mouth while a single chip was being consumed in the left.

The first half of the chip went down well and I cockily popped the other half into my mouth for a repeat performance. Having chewed and swallowed that I found that my mouth was completely empty, and I was transformed from a lad with a reasonable life expectancy to one whose day's - perhaps hours or even minutes - were numbered! I arrived home in

Photo: Reverend Ron Sutton.

A Trinity Square School group c.1934. Many of the children are in the book.
Boy, L back: Ronald Sutton, Boy, R back: John Leigh
Back row: Irene Cunningham, Derek Hodkinson, Geoffrey Campsell, Frank Gaskell, ---- ----, Kenneth Haywood,
Bernard Ratcliffe, Colin Smith, Gerald Bradley, Lilian Oldham
2nd row: Jean Williams, Angela Lawton, Nancy Hadfield, Vera Perry, Joan Howarth, Beryl Frost, Eileen Eaves.
Front row: Nora Swinson, Joyce Charlesworth, Helen Potts, Mary Norton, Margaret Parr, Jean Hackney, Sheila Craghill, Jean Rowbotham.

great distress, my condition obvious to all.

"What's up?", asked Mother. Tears streaming down my face, I replied "I've swallowed my chewing gum!", fully expecting this announcement to produce wide-spread alarm among the family. The last thing I expected from Mother was an accusing, "You've pinched a chip, haven't you?" I nodded woefully. "You've no right!" said Mother, "You should wait till they're on your plate." I couldn't believe this. "But I've swallowed my chewing gum, Mum," I bawled, with sobbing emphasis. If possible my distress was increasing.

"Don't shout at me," said Mother, "and in future keep your fingers to yourself."

I couldn't understand it. Where were the loving arms and the bosom to which I should be clasped at this perilous time? How could one single, solitary chip (admittedly, a long one), which could so easily have fallen from Mrs Livesey's scoop before it reached my basin, be more important than my rapidly ebbing life?

"And what are you scriking for?" asked Mother as she dished out the chips. "I've a good mind to give you a few less for -" She stopped in mid-sentence and slowly ran her eyes over my elder brothers, Tony and Vincent. "Have you two been giving our Geoffrey that rubbish about swallowing chewing gum?" she asked them. Heads were shaken in unison. "Well, somebody has. Geoffrey, come and sit down for your dinner. Come on, you're not going to die and nothing's going to happen to you, you can take that from me. Now, wipe your face. You have been upset, haven't you? Here, there's a few extra chips!"

In the latter half of 1934 I moved from Miss Mitchell's classroom at Trinity to Miss Ingham's for my final year at the school, prior to the move to Daybrook Street. Bespectacled like Miss Mitchell, Miss Ingham had reddish cheeks which hinted exasperation and I felt I needed to be on my guard. Her class did prove to be a stricter regime but this was no bad thing, generally. My desk was between that of Annie Fairbrother and Eileen Eaves. I had a deep, brotherly regard for Annie since neither of us wore anything fancy, and a natural bond developed. Eileen was different; impeccably dressed and with the beauty to match, she was a joy to behold and I retained a shyness towards her.

In the room, near the window, was a doll's house made from matchboxes, and about as functional as Miss Mitchell's glass case of stuffed birds. When Miss Ingham intended to speak for any length of time or required a period of silence we would be instructed to fold our arms or place our hands on our heads. A good idea this since it virtually placed us all in straight-jackets and eliminated fidgeting.

During craft lessons I was taught to knit both plain and purl but preferred to bind milk-bottle tops with raffia. These were joined together to form table mats and were probably sold to boost school funds.

I had one lamentable failure in this class and it haunts me to this day. Miss Ingham had a set of illustrated cards, each posing an arithmetical problem. These cards were introduced in the last few weeks of my stay there. We were each issued with a card, told to study the picture, to read the text carefully, and having solved the problem, to take the card to Miss Ingham's desk and state the answer. Should the answer be correct the card would be changed for another, and so on.

My card showed the front of a house containing several windows, and a series of clues to calculate the number of windows at the back of the house and at the sides. The question being, 'How many windows has the house got in total?' This seemed fairly easy to me and I left my seat, went to the front of the class and presented my card. "Sixteen, Miss", I said.

"Wrong", said Miss Ingham. "Try again."

Try again I did, searching for the error I had made the first time. I failed to find it but dallied before making a further approach to the front. "Sixteen, Miss." "Wrong" said Miss Ingham. "Try again."

For the remainder of that period I puzzled over the mystery and retained the card for another day. The next time we were asked to return to our card problems it was a repeat of the first day performance for me. I could see no alternative to my initial answer and returned to my desk twice more with my window card while other bright sparks in the class were exchanging cards one after another.

Incredible as it may seem, this impasse continued week after week and my embarrassment was increasing with the passing of time. Naturally, I discussed my problem at home with my brother Tony and although he concurred with my answer based on what I had told him, he pointed out, rightfully, that he needed to see the actual card to give a fair judgement as he reckoned ambiguity to be a factor. I declined to 'borrow' the card from school for one night as I believed it would constitute temporary theft, so I remained stuck with the problem right through to the end of my Trinity days. I have always believed Miss Ingham was wrong to allow me to suffer in the way that she did. She should have said, earlier, "Look, Geoffrey,

Looking down Hibel Road earlier this century. The shadowed buildings, left of centre, faced the Town's main railway station.

you're in a rut with this, aren't you. Would you like me to explain where you're going wrong?"

It didn't happen and in the end I was glad to get away from there and take my place in Mrs Cooper's class at Daybrook.

Outside of Victoria Park, while the girls were mainly occupied with their skipping and hopscotch, or with skirt-hems tucked into knickers, practising handstands against walls, one of the boys' main interests was the collecting of and competing for cigarette cards; the compilation of sets was a first priority but spare cards abounded. A popular street pastime was to lean several cards against the angle of a wall and to take turns flicking other cards at them from a kneeling position at the kerb. The cards knocked down were kept by the striker.

Two sporting celebrities depicted on cards of those days whose names appealed to me, I remember, were boxer Larry Mizler and tennis player Dorothy Round.

To remain occupied in play without expense was a must and we were all adept at making paper aeroplanes on a day-to-day basis. The string game known to me now as 'Cat's Cradle' (we didn't have any name for it at all that I can recall) where criss-cross string patterns are transferred from one pair of hands to another was a great favourite. What I called a 'tin-lid twizzle' - another instance of string playing its part - was easily made by punching two holes in a tin lid, each hole about half an inch from the centre and opposite each other, and threaded through with about a yard of string, the ends tied to form a loop. Held with the hands apart, the lid central, it could be quickly 'wound up' and played concertina fashion for as long as the player wished. The spinning disc, when it had a jagged edge, could have been dangerous but prudence prevailed at all times.

Should we acquire a small ball-bearing we would make a 'jumping bean' with a small piece of silver paper, always available from an empty ten or twenty cigarette packet in the gutter. A short silver tube was easily made with a round pencil-end as an aid. One end of the silver paper tube was sealed while still on the pencil. The tube, usually just over an inch in length at this point was removed from the pencil, the ball-bearing inserted and the open end sealed as carefully as possible. the bean was then placed in an empty match-box and rattled to a liquorice torpedo shape. Once made, the bean's antics on a gently manipulated tray were fascinating to watch.

A very clever self-made toy was the military tank made from a cotton bobbin, its rims notched with a pen-knife, a tallow 'washer', an elastic band

and a couple of used matchsticks. The tank's elastic 'motor' was threaded through the bobbin hole, held with a half matchstick at one end across the hole, and threaded through the tallow washer on the other side before being held by a full matchstick which acted as the winder. The tallow - ingenious idea, this - operated as a governor, and slowed movement down giving the tank its characteristic lethargic movement.

Pressing discarded orange peel with a boot or welly in a puddle provided temporary amusement and wonderful colour patterns on the water's surface. Street games also included clay marbles - mibs, we called them - and five-stones which could be purchased cheaply from Natty Whalley's shop in Commercial Road. A set of five-stones comprised four baked and enamelled clay cubes, each with four fluted sides and a ball of similar material. As an indication of size all five pieces could just be grasped in one hand. We would squat in a group on the flags and play in turn, using one hand only. The ball was tossed lightly in the air by the player and a stone was grabbed quickly from the cluster on the pavement before catching the ball. Repeated three more times successfully and the player would be holding all five stones. These were then tossed back into the air, as one, and as many stones as possible caught on the back of the hand and counted as a score.

Natty Whalley's was a dark shop kept by a plump elderly woman who came from out of the darkness at the back of the shop into the half-light. Perhaps she was a widowed Mrs Whalley and her husband had been Nathaniel. That would explain the 'Natty'.

It was a toy shop which catered for the poorer child, with most things either a ha'penny or a penny. One could buy little ball-bearing games; hand-held circular containers with a glass cover which you vibrated gently to coax the balls within to a specific location. There were whistles with a rattling pea inside, goggles and masks and horizontal propellors which could be launched up a spiral wire into the air; 'bombs' primed with explosive caps and sent skywards on the end of a string; non-mechanical potato guns. These were just a short length of brass tubing which one stuck a quarter of an inch into a potato to load and a cast-metal musket-shaped piece that ramrodded out the potato pellet with a 'plop'. Kazoos were very popular particularly at Carnival time. There were magnets and catapults (tu-tangs we called them), pea shooters to be fired from the mouth with black pea ammunition on sale as well, and simple water pistols where the rubber bulb was held in the hand. Tops and whips and skipping ropes could be bought at a number of other outlets as well, including Bob Ashton's mixed shop in the same road. He had a little side window in Fence Street displaying these articles plus other items such as sheets of transfers, yo-yos and carnival streamers - rolls of thin paper ribbon in a variety of colours to be thrown when the Macclesfield Carnival paraded past his shop each year.

Toys of a rather more up-market status could be had from the oddly named 'Dairy' further along the road on the other side. Mrs Whittaker, whose shop it was, supplied a wide range of goods; cap pistols, pea guns, repeater water pistols, balsa gliders with stick and elastic launchers, kites, all manner of push-along and spring-driven toy vehicles including, for sixpence, military tanks with rubber tracks and a gun in the turret spitting fire with each winding. Domestic type playthings for little girls were just as plentiful with babes in baths, cookers, smoothing irons, tea and baking sets, etc. Boxed games such as blow football and board games, draughts, ludo and snakes and ladders were a good selling line too.

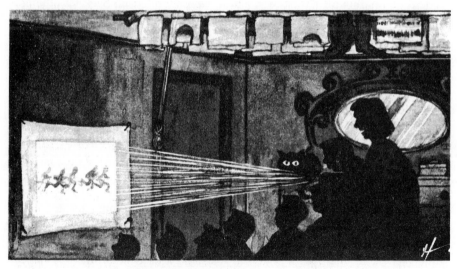

**Film premiere - Waterloo Street style!**

# Chapter Ten
# The cinematograph

Healthy physical outdoor activities were important to all youngsters and the park played its part, and whenever a ball of any size - and shape! - was available, swarms of lads of all ages would be drawn to the rough, dirt surface of the football pitch. A less robust street exercise I favoured was the propelling and steering of a hoop, since traffic was no great problem. Hoops were made of rounded metal and were about forty inches in diameter, which was about my height at the time. Some kids would bowl the hoop along by beating it with a wooden stick, but the right tool for the job was metal also and bent as a hook at the business end. The hoop could then be slurred along with the hook at the back and when going downhill it was necessary to catch the hoop with the hook and use it as a brake. It was good healthy exercise all right.

A team game played regularly by boys was 'Crumtick' - my spelling, as I have never seen the word written before. It was a form of team leap-frog in which the participants often ended up as a heap of humanity, like a collapsed rugby scrum.

Each winter, with the onset of dark nights, we would play Riley-O. Originally, this must surely have been Rally-O, but Riley-O it was. This was a complicated team game of hide and seek on the move, in which the seekers could take prisoners and the hiders could attempt rescue. Our games were usually orchestrated by Harry Newton, a big lad about six years my senior, who lived in Fence Street and was one of my brother Tony's pals. It will be seen from this that Harry Newton had plenty of time for lads younger than himself; not a common trait and therein lay his appeal to me. Tony, Vincent and I returned home one dark night happily wearied by three hours chasing about the streets with Harry and the rest of the gang, and the cries of "Riley-o-o-o-o" and "Give us a wa-a-a-arning" had ceased and would sound again on another exhilarating evening.

We remained bubbly as we prepared for bed and talk was of Harry this, and Harry that, when, unexpectedly, Mother said, "I'd rather you lads didn't play with Harry Newton!" We were astonished by this comment. Not play with Harry Newton? What on earth was Mother talking about?

"It's his face," explained Mother. "I can see mischief in it."

All three of us complained to her at once in support of Harry and bedlam reigned for a time. Mother was left in no doubt how unpopular her observation had been. It is likely, too, that she was impressed by the vehemence we had shown in defence of a friend.

A week or two later Dad came home with a surprise gift for us. He had paid twelve shillings and sixpence for a cinematograph. This important item of entertainment equipment came supplied with two films, each contained in a round tin can. Tony was appointed projectionist and Sunday evening was chosen as film night each week.

On the first night of showing, there was an unusual amount of preparation. Dad pinned a piece of white sheeting to the dividing wall between front room and kitchen, the cinematograph was assembled with no little difficulty on the dining table with one spool stuck up high and the other extending low over the front edge of the table. The projection light was an ordinary torch bulb, its electrical power supplied by an ordinary flat-torch battery with a long and short springy prong sticking out of the top. The whole thing was hand-cranked (by Tony, of course) and transmission was by a looped coiled spring.

The film, 16mm, had to be threaded from the upper spool, through the projection gate and then fed to the receiver spool. All this took time, as did the final adjustments, Dad moving the screen up slightly, the table dragged back a few more inches...... but eventually we were ready for our premiere, eight Hunters and Tum-tum the cat, protected from the fire by our large one-piece fireguard with the brass rail across the top. The gas mantle was turned off and the flickering fire provided its own moving display on walls and ceiling. Tony switched on and commenced to crank away. The first film, which lasted about two minutes, depicted three men moving about in shrubbery on a dark night. We would never have ascertained that from this showing which was nothing more than a murky image of shadows, but we had previously studied the film in daylight and knew its content. Used as we were to the sharp definition of the cinema matinees it was still thrilling to see filmed movement on our own wall, albeit indistinct.

The end of that film resulted in a break in proceedings as the gas mantle was lighted, the film re-wound and the second film threaded. This one we knew would be an improvement being a daytime film of a school sports day showing youngsters engaged in a fifty yards dash, as a finale. And so it proved. Although not terribly clear, there was enough definition to understand the film's content without prior knowledge, and although Tony's cranking showed the sprint race in slow motion ("I wanted to make it last longer") we were well satisfied with this first performance.

The second week's show went well, in terms of speed, and we were able to enjoy each film twice before calling it a night. On the third week we ran into problems. The batteries of those days had limited life and during the showing of the first film the light began to fade. Applying an old idea, we warmed the flat battery in front of the fire for a little while then returned it to its housing in the cinematograph. For a few brief seconds we had brightness and then, rapidly, the light faded to nothingness. Tony was bitterly disappointed by this and with a curt "I'm going out", he grabbed his coat from behind the front door, and went out into the night. The rest of us sat in silence, not knowing what to say, the light from the fire dancing on our faces. There seemed no point in lighting the gas mantle.

After a few minutes Tony returned, his mood buoyant. "Harry says he can fix things up for us to see the films. He says he'll bring something from his house if you'll let him." The suggestion was directed at Mother and in view of her comment some days earlier I didn't know what to expect.

"Tell him if he can do anything to help he'll be very welcome to try," responded Mother.

Out into the night again went Tony and within minutes was back, with Harry Newton, an accumulator and wires dangling from his hand. The gas mantle was lit and Harry fiddled with his bits of wire and in no time at all pronounced everything ready. Tony cranked his way happily to another successful conclusion and following the return of the machine to its box, Harry stayed on and partook of Oxo and a slice of bread, and conducted himself with such commendable decorum that Mother was completely charmed by him and from that point on Harry was welcome at our door and in our home at any time.

A fine photographic study of a Macclesfield Wakes Fair following the First World War. The photographer's camera was poised on the wall outside Central station overlooking the bull-ring area of Waters Green where for many years, until fairly recently, market stalls were stored. By the 1930s a weekly cattle market continued to be held in Waters Green but the amusement fairs in May and at Wakes moved elsewhere.

## Chapter Eleven
## Life was fun

Life was far from dull in those supposedly hard times; rather did I find it an endless stream of interest with all manner of treats extra to the games we played. There were sudden pleasures like the time Dad announced, out of the blue, "We're going to the Circus!" and we put on our coats right away and did just that. Regrettably, there was a sad aspect to this story.

The Circus was on Windmill Street ground which I believe was in regular use as a dog-racing track at that time. Our family group made its way along York Street, crossed Buxton Road and began the gentle climb towards Black Road. We were between Flint Street and Longden Street when a runaway horse with a cart attached came over the canal bridge and raced past us wide-eyed and clearly terrified. We watched its wild descent until it passed out of sight, downwards towards Buxton Road Bridge and Waters Green. We continued to the Circus - it had a lion-taming act, with a cage that took an eternity to assemble and dismantle - but the horse incident had taken the shine off things. We learned later that the poor creature had run itself to its death lower down the road. If only it had been facing uphill when startled there would probably have been a much happier conclusion to the story.

On the odd occasion, given a nice Sunday evening, Dad would arrange with Mr Harold Percival, who lived about a third the way down the left side of Princess Street, for all the family to be taken for a drive. It is a pity I have never been knowledgeable about cars; I could have been more informative. Mr Percival's car was a large vintage something-or-other, with spoked wheels. You didn't get into it, you climbed up and on to it, rather like making a final assault on a summit, and just as exhilarating!

Predictably, we would eventually finish up at some country pub and we kids would lounge on a grassy bank, enjoying Smith's crisps, salted from the blue paper twist, while the folks enjoyed a leisurely tipple. The Percival family included son Harold and daughter Nellie.

The bowling season in Victoria Park provided us all with immeasurable joy when Dad participated. The impression I have now is that my father did not spend much time bowling in a casual, recreational way, but was attracted by the challenge presented by handicap competitions. He was a good bowler and when he entered an event he was in with a chance and we loved to support him. Other names on the sheet usually included Messrs Norman Stanton, Nelson Sidebotham, Bill Lawton, Arnold Axford, Sam Swindells, Ernie Cornes, Harold Brannick (of whom I intend to comment further, later in my story), Albert Capper and Sam Goodier.

When Dad played, we kids would place ourselves at the jack end throughout the game. The making of noise was taboo but our constant moving around the perimeter of the green was accepted without a hint of criticism. On several occasions Dad reached the final and faced Mr Stanton. Mr Stanton, it has to be said, was a man of considerable stature - metaphorically speaking - both as a bowler and as one of Nature's gentlemen. It was not unknown for he and my father to agree choice of prizes before the first jack had been bowled. The prizes, supplied by Ald. Albert Breeze from his jeweller's shop in Sunderland Street, were top quality goods, believe me. The finest trophy won by Dad was a grand-daughter clock. This petite descendant of distinguished stock stood in our home as a monument to our father's prowess throughout the remainder of his life and beyond it.

The calendar played a part in many other pleasures throughout each year. The May and Wakes fair are deserving of mention and I intend to comment on those shortly. There was Easter to anticipate and the traditional chocolate egg to enjoy when it came, and Barnaby, Blackpool and my birthday, which all coincided, and the fruit-picking seasons. Bilberry from Tegsnose had a special appeal for me since the fruit made my favourite pie. I always seemed to be the youngest of the picking group, but I dare say my younger brother, Les, and sister Dot did their bit in later years. The walk to Tegsnose was always a treat. Buxton Road was an attractive route especially at Forest Cottage and the stroll up the old road became increasingly rural in no time at all. The 'salt-box' on the right was always good for a pause. On the crest of the hill a sign advertised ice cream at a farm high on the left. We always fancied going up that hilly bank but we never seemed to have anything to go with so it remained an unfulfilled desire.

Tony and Vincent were prolific bilberry pickers and amassed far more fruit than me. My tentative approach was due to fear of large hairy caterpillars. One early evening when my bilberry tally was embarrassingly small I elected to remain longer when the others were ready to return home. As a result it was dusk when I finally made my way down the last field to the stile and started trudging down the road with the shooting butts on my

Victoria Park: Concerts in the bandstand were welcome and sedate events in the years before World War II

left. Almost at once I saw ahead of me what appeared to be a large pot ornament resting on the stone wall on my right, but as I came abreast of it I was amazed to find it was a barn owl. We faced each other, five feet apart, for about a minute, sharing a silent respect, before I quietly turned and walked softly away. A thrilling experience never to be forgotten.

A few weeks after bilberry picking it would be time to harvest blackberries from Ecton and the canal side, and later in the year conkers and sweet chestnuts (we would walk to Monks' Heath and back for those). The collecting and safeguarding of wood for bonfire night came soon afterwards. Gangs of lads tended to pinch wood from each other as the big night approached. The Big Yard bonfire was a huge event which generated considerable goodwill between neighbours, with a generous willingness by so many to bake potatoes and make treacle toffee and parkin for general consumption.

'Standard' and 'Brock' dominated the firework market with their rockets, Roman candles, Catherine wheels, concertina-shaped rip-raps, Bengal matches and so on.

Christmas afforded pleasurable anticipation, and application also, for each year when the month of December had reached its teens we would beg a suitable cardboard box from a sweet shop, sketch a scene on the lid and carefully prick through the drawing with a needle. All that was then required was a short stub of candle stuck centre-bottom inside the box. With the box held lid facing forward and a heat exit hole centre top, we had a special lantern for our door-to-door carol singing.

Our singing at people's doors was not always appreciated. Many is the boot or some other weighty object thrown at the door by the occupant to signify hostility, and we were quick to heed the message!

For large families such as ours the festive season must have meant a great deal of careful planning and prudent budgeting. Our Xmas pudding was made by Mother several weeks earlier and had a number of thruppeny 'joeys' included in the mixture. Presents had to be bought and secreted (Granny Talbot may well have collaborated in this wise deception) and Christmas fare had to be accumulated.

The artificial Christmas tree and the ornament box were brought down from the top shelf of our living room cupboard. This box also contained the garlands that would loop their way across our ceiling. A fair-sized turkey was a 'must', as was a bottle of John Haig Dimple Scotch whisky, the three-sided bottle encased in gold wire-netting. This was used exclusively for giving tea a seasonal boost - a treat not confined to our parents, I might add.

A turkey we had one year proved to be too large for our oven but Mr Booth, whose bakehouse was between Eastgate and Princess Street, was happy to save the day.

On Christmas Eve stockings with names attached were hung from the fireguard before we retired to bed in a state of excitement. It was difficult to get to sleep on that night and easy to waken in the morning, and we kids would creep downstairs at the first light of dawn to take stock of our newly acquired possessions. Always the stockings would contain an apple and orange and nuts with the bigger gifts on the floor below. I have fond memories of chocolate selection boxes, Cadbury's being my favourite. Priced at half-a-crown they would each contain a variety of fifteen, two ounce chocolate bars. A Meccano set with its tools, construction pieces, screws and nuts and easy to understand diagrams, ranks as the finest joy-creating gift I received in those Waterloo Street years.

Nor was our Christmas joy confined to home for we Hunters were blessed with an additional bonus each year. Mother worked with Mr Harold Brannick, who lived in Hope Street across from our school pals, Raymond and Gerald Bradley. Mr Brannick was a gentleman of some standing within the brethren of Fountain Street Mission. Each year he provided us with tickets to attend the Mission's Sunday School party, held on a Saturday afternoon/early evening. The fact that we attended Sunday School elsewhere didn't seem to matter. Members of the Sinnett family, famous in the town for its fruit and vegetable products, were the benefactors of these wonderful Mission tea parties, and I am happy to pay tribute to them now. Even all these years afterwards I feel the deepest sense of gratitude for the kindness we received at Fountain Street, time after time. 'Charity', in the minds of the Sinnett family, Mr Brannick, and all those around him at that time was the beautiful word it was always intended to be.

Our short walk along York Street, across Buxton Road and up the long entry short-cut to the Mission was, each year, a stroll of joyous anticipation; a sense of sweet expectation never to be denied.

A superb tea party was always followed with a concert. I well remember Mr Brannick and several other gentlemen stretched across the stage singing 'Uncle Tom Cobleigh and all'. A young lady, a stranger to me at that time, with knapsack on her back, melodiously informed her audience how happy she was when she was hiking, and a white-apron-clad chap, knotted handkerchief on his head, wielded a broad, dry, decorator's brush and sang:

> "Slap, dash, slap, dash, in and out the corners,
> Talk about a Fancy Ball;
> I put more white-wash on the old woman
> Than I put upon the garden wall!"

I have had to wait sixty years to learn that the singing hiker was Mr Brannick's daughter, Marion - still strutting about life's stage, I'm pleased to report - and the brush wielding chap was her Uncle Charlie. Marvellous!

A concert highlight for me was supplied by a little chap of five or six years of age named Neville Thomas. Neville had an assortment of costumes, a most attractive puckish face, the confidence of a seasoned pro, and he sang with relish. I have never forgotten Neville and his 'Changing of the Guard'.

To conclude these parties we were given a take-home bag which always included a pack of figs. "Good working medicine', declared Mother. It seems Mr Brannick and Company thought of everything.

The May and Wakes fairs were always a great source of pleasure for me, even with an empty pocket. Always welcomed by my group was the arrival of the dodgems ride which occupied centre spot in the Waters before the Mont Blanc ride competed for the space. Not because of its accepted amusement value, since it was mainly an adult entertainment, but because the huge double-decker trailer used to transport the cars was kept parked on the waste ground alongside the railway wall opposite Arighi Bianchi's store in Commercial Road before cattle pens were installed there. Once a bunch of us lads had climbed on board we could be sailing the Spanish Main within moments.

At the fair itself I loved the loud thrilling sound of steam organs, the brightly painted roundabouts, swings and 'big boats', the coconut shies, stalls selling unshelled peanuts and brandy snaps ('London Curl' some chose to call them), vendors with their furry toy monkeys, bats with elastic-attached lurex balls, the colourful 'windmills' on sticks and soft papier-mache birds with tails that spun and whistled in the breeze.

Against this background I could join the crowd which enjoyed, for free, the tongue-in-cheek audacity of the side-show barkers, witness the disputes at the roll-a-penny stalls or be mesmerised by the small coloured celluloid balls rising and falling on fluctuating jets of water at the rifle range, which always had easier target columns of white clay pipes. The boxing booth with its back to the Waters Green Tavern was something of a free show, too, as the various fighters were introduced to the crowd outside the booth and challenges issued to all-comers. Pugilist 'Nipper' Plant of Hanley was a regular and there was ample evidence that 'cauliflower ears' were a feature of fact rather than of fiction.

I enjoyed, mostly, the coconut shies on the patch of level ground at the top of the slope where participants had their backs to Central Station. They would first select, from a long-legged crate, the wooden ball missiles by 'weighing' them in their hands, and insist on more sawdust between shie stands and coconuts atop them. Steel sheets, suspended behind the shies and regularly white-washed, would toll a knell each time a target was missed, which was far more often than not. Winners, allowed the right to step over the toe-board and collect their coconut prize, would shake several close to an ear to assess the milk content, before making their choice. With many this was pseudo chest-beating I am sure, but why not? There was little enough to crow about in those days.

Father ensured we added coconut to our diets at these times. Always, year after year, perhaps in common with many other families, we would use a hot poker to gain access to the coconut milk via one of the three 'eyes'. This proved to be quite unnecessary. Years later I was to learn that one coconut eye is umbilical, and contains nothing but the soft flesh of the kernal and can be penetrated with any fine implement. A wooden meat skewer would have been ideal. We live and learn.

Who of us, remembering those days, could ever forget the appetising smell of soft-fried potato pieces emanating from the little stall close to Buxton Road railway bridge? Especially during the Wakes Fair when the evenings were dark and the stall was all aglow; and year after year the same stocky little couple busied themselves over their hot stove and wove a piece of magic into the tapestry of the times.

**Daybrook Boys' School just prior to its demolition in the 1960s. The school railings had been sacrificed for the war effort over 20 years earlier and the author has drawn in how the entrance to the school appeared in the 1930s.**

## Chapter Twelve
## Daybrook School

It seems likely to me that the Barnaby holiday of one year in the mid-thirties was one where we were forced to give Blackpool a miss. Tony had earlier joined the Macclesfield 20th St Andrew's Wolf Cub pack, located in the Barracks Square, Crompton Road, the scout and cub master being Mr Adam Hope who had a scout shop in Chestergate. During his tenderfoot period with the pack, Tony took a few coppers each week as savings towards a cub uniform, and in due course he attended Mr Hope's shop to be fitted out. Words like 'neckerchief' and 'woggle' were added to our vocabulary, and the oath, which began "I promise to do my best, to do my duty to God and the King ....." was added to our mental library. Tony looked quite smart in his green cap with the yellow piping and the wolf cub badge, the green jersey and non-elastic green garters which had small black buckles to adjust tension and dangled down from his stockings on each side like the ribbons of a rosette.

It is likely that he was accompanied on his long walk to the Barracks each week by Jack Wooliscroft of Fence Street. Whether Eric Simpson, or Sandy Melvin, likely lads close to us, were involved I cannot say, but in due course both Tony and Jack put down their names for summer camp at Bolton-le-Sands, and my folks decided that the whole family would attend the camp on Visitors' Day on Wednesday of that particular week. And so, Tony and Jack and the rest went off happily on their great adventure and early on the following Wednesday it was the family's turn to make the trip.

Bolton-le-Sands, close to the Lake District, was no mean feat for those times as a day excursion, but the seven of us, the youngest, Dorothy, a mere three-year-old, managed it cheerfully. The journey to Lancaster was by train and I recall, vaguely, having to cross Manchester from London Road to Exchange Station. At Lancaster we hopped on a bus for the few extra miles to the camp and it began to rain heavily and our spirits sank. Then, what seemed to be a miracle happened, and in the space of a few hundred yards we moved out of a rain-soaked area into one of complete dryness with accompanying sunshine. The fine weather stayed with us for the rest of the day. Tony, we found, was enjoying camping life and revelling in the bracing sea air.

Visitors' day was also sports day at the camp and having won a foot race, Jack Wooliscroft was given a bag of chocolate biscuits as his prize, each wrapped in plain silver paper. Generously, he handed them round. Again, like the chocolate digestive biscuit given to me at school, this was a chocolate biscuit to remember for ever. Having sucked off the thick chocolate coating, the inner biscuit was a firm, pliable, chewy delight the like of which they simply do not make today. Thanks for the memory, Jack! My family's return to Macclesfield was uneventful.

It was in the second half of 1934 that I and the other boys in my group moved from Trinity Square to Daybrook Street, lessening my journey to school to a mere 200 yards or so. I was on very familiar ground here as I was already attending Sunday School classes in the Daybrook building and the Mission services in the evening.

Before returning to the subject of day-to-day schooling I feel I have a duty, at this point, to refer to the Sunday School aspect of my life at that time. It would be true to say that the Sabbath was my least favourite day of the week, mainly because it was obligatory to spend most of that day wearing my best suit, and this had a great restraining effect on me. No trees could be climbed; no walls could be scaled; no pavement flags could be sprawled upon and any spot I felt a need to rest my bottom had to be first scrutinized for dryness and an acceptable degree of cleanliness. It was a day for all to dress up and in the morning I would watch the arrival of the smart Fence Sunday School congregation, many of that number familiar faces, seen on that day only but on a regular basis.

Daybrook Street Sunday School was a more relaxed regime. Mr Evans - 'Pop', we affectionately called him - was the lay-preacher. He lived in the little Almshouse complex on Buxton Road. He had several good people in support. Young Mr Arthur Morlidge of Blagg Street was my class teacher, and the Weaver family of Waterloo Street was well represented also. Mr & Mrs Bailey (from the Beech Lane area) officiated as well and always brought their sons Tom and Bert with them. Many is the delightful country walk I enjoyed with the Baileys after classes and they are remembered with great affection.

Field treats, whether by barge on the canal or by train, and Christmas tea parties, were highlights of each year. Mr Evans had charge of the Band of Hope class on Monday evenings as well, where emphasis was placed on the evils of demon drink, and we would sing songs from our long, thin red books. Typical of these was the one which had as its chorus:

Temperance boys and girls are we,
Temperance boys, temperance girls;
Temperance boys and girls are we,
Always true we mean to be.

We would recite such things as, "Look not upon the wine when it is red .....Alas, it biteth like a serpent and stingeth like an adder."

They were happy gatherings and always there was a period at the end of each meeting when those who wished could recite or sing their own favourite piece. Arthur Morlidge deserves special mention for his good work at that time and for his dedication from that point on. For most of his working life he was employed by Colliers at their foundry in King Edward Street. He had a great sense of fellowship and was totally devoted to Hurdsfield Church and its associated activities. That was Arthur's life, right to its end, and I am sure God never had a truer servant than he.

Daybrook Street School was a sturdy Gothic-type structure built entirely of stone. It had a small raised forecourt enclosed in railings. Younger boys were segregated in the ground floor classrooms while the older ones - the ones intending to remain there until they reached working age - occupied the upper floor. Mr Brocklehurst was headmaster, but since he evidently had his hands full aloft I saw little of him in my four years there - or of Mr Cunningham who also taught upstairs. Mrs Cooper, a well-built lady who had been at the school many years, received each new intake from Trinity and had charge of classes 1 and 2 combined, and coped well, and at the time I joined her Vincent and Tony were in Mr Timothy Doggert's class 3 and Mr Ernest Baker's class 4, respectively. My class had been used to calling our three former teachers 'Miss' but Mrs Cooper insisted she be addressed as 'Mum', which took a bit of getting used to since I already had a special mum in my life. I recall the care I took during those first few days writing on the first page of each exercise book determined to avoid any ink blots, to spell every word neatly and correctly and to ensure every sum was correct. Having taken such care on each first page it seemed sacrilege to have to be expected to write on the reverse side!

My contemporaries will recall those exercise books on the back of which was written a piece of wisdom which began: 'When you leave school, do not think your education has finished; it has only just begun....." There was also a set of tables to assist our calculations, pertaining to weight, volume and distance. It was Mrs Cooper who transformed our printed style of writing into a flowing hand. We also read aloud, individually, and were constantly reminded that the 't' in often was silent as in the word 'soften' (were Mrs Cooper alive today she would have cause for much complaint). Singing in attempted unison was a welcome feature of our life then. On one occasion Mrs Cooper cocked an ear to my mouth during one of these sessions and said, "You're a puzzle to me, Hunter. You talk like a bogey-man and yet sing so sweetly." The latter part of her comment pleased me no end since it was in complete contrast to the opinion of others.

Storytime was my favourite period when Mrs Cooper settled herself at her desk and brought children's classics to life. We enjoyed The Water Babies and Black Beauty in their turn but it was The Wizard of Oz which really captured my full attention. The written word had a special charm which the Metro-Goldwyn-Mayer film a few years later - brilliant as it was - failed to capture for me and it is the memory of the book I prefer to retain all these years later. In this class we were also introduced to mythology and the Trojan Horse and the Romulus and Remus stories were also well received.

It was about this time that I qualified for free clogs and school dinners as did Vincent and several other lads also. As twelve noon approached each day teachers would hand out dinner tickets from a roll quite openly. I accepted this openness without qualms but Vincent would have preferred a more covert method of distribution.

Monday to Friday then, our little group would leave Daybrook at 12 noon and walk to the clinic at Pierce Street. The 108 steps was a regular climb for us to get to the market place, and having reached Leach's chemist shop (where Gibbs dentifrice was constantly promoted in the window) we would cross over Mill Street into Stanley Street, passing on the corner the long-established apothecary and drysalter business of Mr Charles Hadfield.

Soon, the pavement, strewn with maize from the corn merchant, would bring us to Cleaver's shop where we had been fitted with our clogs, and Mr Ernie Hall's barber shop where our hair was regularly cropped close to the head leaving just a canopy-style tuft at the front. There was nothing fancy about Mr Hall's saloon. Sawdust-filled spittoons were placed about the floor and it was, predominantly, a shaving establishment. Hall senior was assisted by his son who I likened to Stan Laurel.

Having passed the Conservative Club we would cross the street to look in Lee's music shop window. Accordions were the most exotic instruments on display. Nearer the scope of our ambitions was the assortment of Hohner harmonicas (mouth organs, to us) and nearer still, bone clappers, black or white, sixpence per pair, and jew's harps of all sizes with a starting price of fourpence for the smallest. Sheet music abounded. The Lees had a boy, Leonard, who though but a youngster like myself, was a fine musician. Today, Leonard lives in West Sussex and is fondly remembered.

Crossing Derby Street we would soon find ourselves in Church Street West which seems hardly to have changed at all and to this day retains the stone sets of bygone years. From there it was a matter of yards only to the entrance we used at the rear of the clinic. It was a bright place being well-windowed and was attended by a large number of boys. Like us they were all noticeably poor and gentian violet, commonly in use then as an antiseptic for skin infections was much in evidence on hands or faces. The meals were quite good. A typical one would start with a soup which usually had two or three butter beans floating in it, then sausage and mash followed by a stodgy rice pudding, well-sweetened and well received.

The route back to school was varied slightly. Once in the market place we would keep left of the church, call at the Gents, up the steps by the old butter market, then read the police notices signed by Chief Constable, Henry Sheasby, before descending the steps down to Robinson Brown's factory at the commencement of Gas Road.

That first year at Daybrook was eventful in the nicest way. The celebration of the Silver Jubilee of King George V and Queen Mary in May, 1935 was a heartening prospect for all, but we Hunters were to enjoy a more personal triumph. Tony, who had exhibited a rare intelligence in those earlier thirties years entered and passed the entrance exams to the Central School and King's School in quick succession, with distinction. What a wonderful fuss there was and how proud we all were of Tony when news of the King's School scholarship became known. It was a considerable shot in the arm for Trinity and Daybrook and from that time on our family enjoyed a new status which was never to diminish.

Tony spent a brief period at Central School, before taking his place at King's, and witnessed the end of Mr Barry's reign as headmaster and the arrival from Croydon of Mr R A Houseman who replaced him. Former pupils of Mr Houseman's regime at Central may find this hard to believe; nevertheless it is true that R A H was so impressed by Tony's King's success and took such a liking to the lad during that summer, that whenever a Granelli's bell was heard, he would hand Tony tuppence and request he purchase two ice cream wafer sandwiches to enjoy together in his study. Such benevolence was not forthcoming to Vincent or me when we attended that school in later years, I can tell you!

The Daybrook celebration of the Royal Silver Jubilee was unexpectedly lavish and far preferable to lessons. On that May morning with the approach of noon, we were presented with commemorative mugs, told to take them home for safe keeping, and to return in the afternoon for the celebrations. On returning to school we were treated to a sumptuous tea party, graced with plenty of swiss buns. For me it was like a fantastic dream come true. Nor was that all. Later we trooped, crocodile style, across town via Sunderland Street and Park Lane to the Premier Picture House in Vincent Street.

The main feature of our film show was 'A Natural Born Salesman' which starred American comedian Joe E Brown, famous for his out-size mouth. So immersed was I in the euphoria of the day that when we returned to Daybrook later and were dismissed, I arrived home convinced I had attended an afternoon matinee and that the time was about 5pm. In fact it was 9pm. Such was the joy of the day.

In that same year we were given a day's holiday when the school was used as a polling station in a General Election. In the evening we sang, "Vote, vote, vote for Mr Remer, he's the favourite of the lot!" He was, too, having been the Town's MP since the end of the Great War.

## Chapter Thirteen
## Daybrook schoolfriends

As I grew older in those thirties years, measured by birthdays and class standards at school, I was attracted more and more to artistic creations. I could always sketch quite well but due to cramped home conditions I had a greater desire to enjoy the work of others rather than to seek to achieve anything myself. The Macclesfield Times junior column, conducted by Auntie Hilda, held regular art and literary competitions from its offices in Queen Victoria Street, and many of the children's entries were displayed each week in the front window. Visits there became a feature of my Saturday morning peregrinations.

My routine would commence about 10 o'clock when I would stroll down Eastgate and the short stretch of King Street to Billington's newsagent's side window where all the paper-back books were displayed. It was a wholly masculine window with a Boys' Own flavour to most of the items on show. 'Mellifont' books predominated, all with a colourful cover, and good tales they were too, judged by the few that found their way to our house. Books on regular display, taking centre stage as it were, were the French Foreign Legion stories of P C Wren, graphically illustrated on the covers with legionnaires, sand, palm trees and violence of one form or another. Callow lad that I was I used often wonder how it was that an ordinary police constable knew so much about the Foreign Legion!

My next call was at the Cinema where, at that time, incidentally, they had in the foyer a Shirley Temple perfume dispenser fixed to the back wall. For an inserted penny the ladies would be sprayed, from a little nozzle, with a little of the contraption's scented contents. Never having witnessed the dispenser operating my pals and I had lifted each other up in turn to sniff at the nozzle to ascertain just what Miss Temple smelt like, and we were suitably impressed.

Every few weeks the Cinema would display on its forecourt, supported by a small easel, a poster advertising the children's matinee programme. My interest was not so much what was going to be 'on' - I'd be going, anyway - but to admire the slick work of the artist, whoever he was. Those posters were marvellous to behold; multi-coloured masterpieces done at speed - you could tell that by the rough pencil work still visible in the background. A pity the Cinema didn't hire the man on a regular weekly

**Daybrook Street School 1936**

Back row (L to R): Leslie Mathers, Roy Hall, Frank Gaskell, Geoffrey Campsell, Bernard Ratcliffe, Fred Slater
2nd row: Harry Blower, John Leigh, Kenneth Haywood, Arthur Priest, Brian Surtees, Derek Wilson, Herbert Lomas
3rd row: Geoffrey Hunter, Roland Heywood, Ronald Sutton, Willie Paramore, George Bailey, Roy Ball, Kenneth Shatwell, Colin Smith
Front row: Gerald Bradley, Derek Roberts, Eric Lynch, Bernard Frith, Kenneth Farr, James Kirkham.

*Photo Rev Ron Sutton*

basis; I'd have had that much more pleasure.

Then off I'd go through a busy bottom market in the Waters, pausing at the book stall facing Prout's tobacconist before making my way up Queen Victoria Street to the Times office. The judging of the art entries puzzled me most of the time. There would be, for example, animals painted beautifully by lads of 11 or 12, but the prizes usually went to younger artists whose work appeared to me to be not very special. The truth is that Auntie Hilda and her colleagues recognised copied work when they saw it and were discerning enough to appreciate the charm of the younger children's spontaneity. I've no doubt that what I considered 'not very special' then, would enchant we tremendously today. Good for Auntie Hilda!

With the merging of classes at Daybrook new friends were made: Eric Stevenson, Tom Broderick, Willie Parramore and Wilf Woodward are remembered fondly. From Henbury, where his father was reputed to have riding stables, came Philma Goddard who was horse-mad and displayed a rare gift for sketching those splendid creatures as well - no mean feat at any age. Also from the Henbury area came Herbert Lomas and his younger brother, Frank. Their father had died and they and their mother came to live in Arbourhay Street. They were a friendly pair who referred to toffee as 'tosh' and when they had any tosh of their own were happy to share it. A nice touch to this tale is that a year or so later Mrs Lomas married Harold Rose, the Granelli salesman who was robbed of his ice cream earlier in my story.

It is likely that homework demands made upon Tony by the masters at King's School resulted in his leaving St Andrew's cubs and at some point afterwards Vincent and I joined the pack together with Harry Blower whose family enjoyed free gas lighting in the front upstairs bedroom of their corner house in Fence Street, the gas lamp being just outside their front door.

As with the school dinner journey, we varied the route going to and from the Barracks Square, Crompton Road, by walking directly up Park Lane on the outward journey and returning home down Crompton Road, Norbury Street and Peter Street, through the ginnel to West Bond Street, then the length of Roe Street and down Queen Victoria Street and home. On this homeward journey each week we frequently broke into song and always chose Roe Street for a loud rendering of 'Wagon Wheels', a popular western number of the times.

Mr Hope was a good scout leader and kept us occupied in the hut we used which I believe had some industrial use as well. It was a dusty place with a distinct odour. Most of the lads lived nearby. Reg Morris actually lived in the square and the other cubs included Len Johnson, Billy Miller, Roy Booth, Sidney Keeble, Ken Bennett, Frank Lawton, Geoffrey and Norman Wilson, Willie Storer, Philip Barber and Gordon Harrison, whose father was a Bond Street butcher who supplied many a potato pie supper for us. We were taught cub promises, cardinal points of the compass, an assortment of knots and semaphore among other things and enjoyed beano evenings in the Scout Hut, West Bond Street, which included film shows of Felix the Cat. We sold tablets of Palmolive toilet soap for cub funds and camped for one weekend at Hawkshead and for a full week at Rhuddlan, North Wales, where prunes were served for breakfast each day but, thankfully, were not obligatory.

One story of St Andrew's Cubs surfaces more than any other. One evening, having completed our official cub duties and expecting a period of games to follow ('O'Grady' was very popular at the time), Mr Hope announced that a treat was in store for us. That evening a concert was being held in St Andrew's School and since some of the artistes were Rover Scouts - Alan Wood, who had a strong theatrical bent was one of them - we cubs had been invited to attend free of charge. Given my love of the theatre this news was manna from heaven for me and I positively bounced down Crompton Road as we marched in single file to the school.

The show had commenced when we got there and the only light came from the stage and as we entered we were invited to climb up onto seating stacked right at the back of the hall giving us a good vantage point. No sooner were we settled and ready to enjoy the show than Mr Hope came strolling along quietly in the half light, peering up at each member of his pack as he passed. On reaching me he paused and raised himself on his toes to get a closer look at me and studied me intently in the dismal light. He then glanced quickly at Vincent on my left, tapped him on the knee with his hand and said, "Vincent, this brother of yours is tired. Come on, get him off home!" I began to plead to stay but Mr Hope cut short my mild protestation. "Now there's a good lad. Don't argue; do as you are told. I know what's good for you." With that he reached up, grabbed each of us by an arm, steered us down to floor level and ushered the pair of us out of the hall. Vincent was livid - so was I, come to that. "What did you have to look tired for?" he asked me. "I didn't, I didn't," I pleaded. "You must have yawned or something," Vincent insisted. "I didn't, I didn't ....."

And so it went on, all the way home, Vincent condemning and I insisting I'd never been more awake in all my life. And that, I believe to this day, was the truth of the matter. There were no wagon wheels rolling along Roe Street that night!

Like a conjurer with a trick to fall back on I have kept a couple of cards up my sleeve as I reach the conclusion of my family's stay at 89 Waterloo Street. Face cards, actually. Two characters, each with a story of 1936, and each of those stories a glowing beacon of remembrance in my boyhood years. Mr Swindells was my family's Provident agent. A smart, military looking man with bright eyes and a neatly trimmed moustache, he was one of several club men who called regularly at my home on Friday evening each week. A family man, he lived in Chadwick Terrace. His son Harold and daughter Alice were talented musicians. When the news reached us that Alice - just 14 years of age - had won the Piano-Accordion playing Championship of Great Britain it was as if one of our own family had been successful. What joy there was in our home! It was a remarkable success enjoyed by Alice, her family and friends and a major triumph for Macclesfield itself. Pride in her achievement has remained with me ever since.

In due course Alice turned professional and as Alicia Dells served with ENSA throughout World War II and continued as an entertainer afterwards.

Now I come to Norman Sutton, another dear old pal. Norman lived within yards of the top of Waterloo Street. He was akin to my brother Tony in age. A decent, dependable lad, I looked up to him, and his family and mine were very close. His Grandad Sutton was a cobbler whose workshop was reached via an entry in lower Hurdsfield Road leading to the rear of Hopwood's greengrocery shop, and thence by a set of wooden steps. But I digress; Norman was a Daybrook pupil also and was a member of the school's soccer team. Early in 1936 that was hardly a claim to fame. Daybrook had had a long barren period in its annual bid to win Macclesfield's Schools' Soccer Trophy, known at that time as the Crew Cup. Upstairs at Daybrook where Mr Cunningham, who also acted as Sportsmaster, and Headmaster Mr Brocklehurst completed the older boys' education, there was a large sepia-tint photograph, high up on the wall, depicting the school's last soccer team to win the local schools' title. It was dated 1911! In the few years that I had shown interest in the contest Central School and Athey Street School monopolised the event with Daybrook,

Mill Street, St George's and St Paul's, etc, making up the numbers.

Well, in due course the annual competition commenced and Daybrook got off to a winning start with sound play, and this purple patch continued to the point where, miraculously it seemed to me, they reached the final with Athey Street going through in the other half of the draw. These were exciting days for Daybrook. Norman and his team-mates, selected from a very limited choice - Eric Frith, Bill Hall, John Boulton, Alan Buckley and Jack Wood are the only names I can recall now - had earned their status, but I remained uneasy. The Athey Street goalkeeper was George Tovey who, throughout their games had appeared unbeatable to me.

On the night of the final at the Puss Bank ground which flanked the canal at Buxton Road, the pendulum of power swung decisively to the side of the under-dogs. Daybrook, in their dark blue strip with the bold white chevron front and back, played out of their skins and George Tovey was found to be fallible after all! A 3-1 victory, I think it was, and I was over the moon.

Through the years Norman Sutton has personified the entire Daybrook team for me. I see him often and always I experience the resounding joy of that incredible evening. Today, having completed a working life on the railway, Norman lives quietly with his wife Lilian. It seems fitting to me that their cottage, above the canal bridge on Buxton Road is just yards from where, more than 60 years ago, an impossible dream came true.

## Chapter Fourteen
## Moving home

Later in that same year, news was received from Macclesfield Corporation that my family's application to return to Hurdsfield Estate had been successful and we were offered the keys to number 3 Crew Avenue. My parents went to take a look at the house one evening - nights were still light at the time - and returned to report that, on the whole, they were greatly pleased with what they had seen. The house itself was a big improvement on our present abode with three bedrooms and a bathroom and red composition floors downstairs that Cardinal polish would work wonders with. It had a front garden, hedged with privet and containing rhododendrons, and a garden at the back with a rockery of lupins, London pride and white rock; a lawn fringed with nasturtians, and a generous expanse for more active gardening containing three apple trees.

And therein lay disappointment. These three apple trees were evidently mature occupants of the garden but until recently there had also been two more much younger trees with a full and long life ahead of them. These had been sawn down, much to my parents distress, and lay where they had been felled. Just who could have perpetrated so dastardly an act was a matter for conjecture, but it was certainly a possibility, and nothing more than that, that the previous occupants of the house had planted the trees themselves and had adopted a 'scorched earth' policy on their departure, not wishing another family to benefit from their investment. Mother kept her thoughts to herself and would only say, "Whoever did that deed will never prosper". Like most folk my mother believed in divine retribution and was happy to leave it at that.

The move to our new home took about a fortnight to arrange and was planned to finalise on a Saturday morning. Early in the evening of our final night in Waterloo Street, I stood at our doorway in pensive mood, looking down the street to savour for the last time the ritual of Welch's docile cart horses coming round the corner from Dicken Street, another coal-delivering day completed, their harness jingling merrily, hooves clattering deliciously on the stone sets as they made their way to Buxton Road and then Lime Grove for the pasture flanking the canal. And behind them, as the perspective of the street diminished to Commercial Road, a hill on the skyline overlooking Gas Road and Hibel Road, with several lofty and

Commercial Road, probably early 1950s, leading towards Gladstone Square. The shops in the 1930s were:
1. Palins grocery and bakers shop adjacent to the Woodman Inn (Mr Joe Buxton, landlord) on the corner of Norton St
2. Holland's hardware and gardening equipment. 3. Miss Bellamy, ladies wear and sub-post office. 4. Natty Whalley's toy shop.
5. Mrs Dean, sweets and tobacconist. 6. Mr Jack Rowbotham, gents hairdresser. 7. The door to the men's reading room, upstairs.

leafless trees on its crest. Grey, independent images they were, with the dark smudges of rooks' nests in the top-most branches. Etched against a sombre industrial sky, they stood like tall, gaunt sentinels of a future beyond.

My memory of the move next day is minimal. I have no recollection of a major upheaval but, clearly, things could not have been too smooth since the giant mangle went with us! I do recall, with crystal clearness, the last minutes at number 89. It was approaching noon and the last of the stuff had been taken and only my mother and me remained. Progressively, throughout the morning she had become less and less talkative and more and more distant. Now, she locked the front door from within and placed the key in her handbag. Slowly she walked into the kitchen and standing in the middle of the room which had been the hub of her domestic life, she took a final look at it, pivoting anti-clockwise on gently shuffled feet.

She contemplated the middle door, the cellar door, the stairs and back door, now denuded of its roller-towel, the back window and the remaining blank walls. Mother, I knew, was in a state twixt past and present and I might as well have been on the other side of the world. Then she lowered her head and began sobbing. I was greatly moved by this but felt any speech an intrusion, so I waited. Her tears and whatever emotions accompanied them lasted but a single minute. Having dried her eyes, she opened the back door and transferred the key from inside to out. I took this as my cue to leave and passed through into the yard. Mother followed, locking the door behind her, placing this key in her handbag also. Then, still without comment, she walked down the yard's narrow pavement towards the entry leading to Dicken Street and beyond, with me in her wake a stride or two behind. A new door was opening for us now. And a new life.

The change of family home came towards the end of my two years in Mrs Cooper's class. It had been expected by my group that when we moved up to class 3 we would be taught by Mr Timothy Doggart but Mr Doggart chose that point to enter retirement, prematurely, I suspect, for he had not enjoyed the best of health. From my new address I made a point of 'calling for' classmate Colin Smith on my way to school each morning. This simple habit was not as inconsequential as it seemed at the time for Colin, a cheerful, easy-going character, was to influence my destiny. The Smith's lived in Smyth Street, a short link between Hurdsfield Road and Arbourhay Street, and were the only family I knew on that right-hand side. There was George, Nora, Colin, Ron and Frank and there may have been younger ones also. They lived opposite the Barlows, the Friths and the Roberts and I retain fond memories of that cosy little street and its occupants.

For a time we boys in class 3 had a sequence of temporary teachers, all male, none of whose names I recall now. At this stage in our education a part of each day was spent singing in unison our multiplication tables up to twelve times twelve and I was sufficiently keen to spend time at home in pursuit of perfection in this art. Time well applied, I might add. I remain troubled to this day by the memory of an incident involving the third sequence teacher. He conducted our examinations and very thorough he was too. We had composition, dictation, geography, history and mental arithmetic, in turn, and as the papers were checked, the results and an individual rating were published and pinned to the classroom wall. With arithmetic, proper, the last of the subjects to come I noted with pride I was running neck and neck in the lead with Ronald Sutton, Derek Wilson and Philip Harding.

We sat this final subject the next afternoon. During lunchtime the master had been busy, for when we took our seats on returning from dinner, he simply turned the blackboard around to display the questions relating to gallons, pints and gills, hundredweights, quarters and pounds, yards, feet and inches, pounds, shillings and pence, with vulgar fractions thrown in for good measure.

After a time, perhaps bored with overseeing us from the front, the master left his desk and quietly stretched his legs in the approved manner by gently moving up and down the aisles. I sensed his approach from behind me on my left and then, out of the corner of my eye noted his feet had come to a stop by my side. Then his right hand brushed the left side of my face and rested on my exercise book, the index finger pointing to a pounds, shillings and pence multiplication sum I had completed earlier. His soft voice in my ear murmured, "I think you should check that again." Then he moved on. I felt bound to obey him and without realising the full implication of what had happened I corrected the error I found and warmed towards him for his kindness.

Two days later when the final results were posted on the wall I was listed at the very top and calculated that without the help I had received I would probably have been in third place. Inwardly, I was devastated by this but kept my shame to myself and after school wandered about Victoria Park alone, reluctant to go home. In the end I reasoned that my own silence on the matter would ensure no spurious praise would come my way. Nor did it and I was grateful for that, but the awful memory of it lingers on.

Following this unhappy episode, Mr Norman Tattersall arrived and took over our class on a permanent basis and stability returned. Young, bespectacled and with auburn hair that bloomed above his head like a newly opened flower, Mr T was a first-class teacher who pushed us fairly hard throughout each week but allowed us to relax and let our hair down on Friday afternoons. We would swop classrooms with Mrs Cooper - that's where the piano was, you see - and we would have a merry old sing-song. An accomplished pianist, Mr T would encourage us through an extensive repertoire of traditional songs, sea shanties and negro spirituals, and persuade a few of us to sing solo at the front of the class. I have no doubt this experience did wonders for my confidence and I shall always be grateful to him for that.

Two more lads who joined the class at that time were Kenneth Shatwell who had Bollington connections, and Roy Ball, newly arrived in Macclesfield. The parents of Roy and his elder brother Alan, were to earn themselves a considerable reputation in the town as proprietors of the chippie at 13 Hibel Road, my own mother being ever eager to sing their praises.

Crew Avenue, off Brocklehurst Avenue, was a cul-de-sac widened at the closed end to allow vehicles to turn. It contained twenty or more houses, their brick surfaces rendered in pebble-dash. The broad pavements were graced with grass patches and hawthorn trees.

It took some time to get to know most of the dwellers there but when my family arrived at number three, the Henshalls with daughter May and son Harry were in the first house, the Houghtons with children Lily, Alec, Mary, Jessie, Tommy and Ethel, at number five followed by the Dakins (to be replaced by the Gregorys soon afterwards), and the Wrights, of whom young John and his sister Doreen were nearest to my age. Lower down still came the Liveseys who had kept the chippie, lower Buxton Road, and the Hunters - no relation to us, but I would have been happy to be so bonded - and the Cundiffs with lads Maurice, Victor, Philip and Peter and two girls whose names elude me right now.

Directly across the avenue from us lived the Lynches with son Eric and daughter Norma at number two. The Heaths, and the Parrs with daughter Margaret, followed on. Mr Henshall and his wife were into their sixties, I should think. He, if not yet retired from the railway was close to it. He was immensely proud of his railway watch which was chain-secured and rested comfortably in his waistcoat pocket. Of the Houghtons, Alec, a

Commercial Road showing the opening to Fence Street on the extreme left.

few years older than me had great versatility. Friendly and industrious, he played the mouth organ with great panache and had a penchant for making trucks - flat-board vehicles equipped with a brake and steered by a rope tied to each end of the front axle. Ours was very much a Tom Sawyer/Huck Finn relationship with many a campfire shared on the tip between Brocklehurst and Nicholson Avenues.

Throughout the 1930s up to the time of King George V's death in 1936, my family's life in the upper reaches of Waterloo Street had not been greatly influenced by the run of shops which extended from lower Hurdsfield Road, through Gladstone Square and along Commercial Road to where Leah's Steam Bakery stood on the corner of Queen Street. Whilst, through the years, incidental purchases were made by us along this 300 yards or so stretch, in the main it served merely as an animated backdrop to our lives since a regular weekend sortie into town and the little shops close by us and Buxton Road businesses supplied most of our needs. The move from Waterloo Street to Crew Avenue, although little more than a quarter of a mile in distance, changed our lives completely. It meant more than a change of house; we now had a change of grocer, greengrocer, butcher, baker, chip shop, newsagent and hairdresser as this busy thoroughfare became more meaningful to us. And with change came choice also, for most types of business were either duplicated, triplicated and even quadrupled, come to think of it, when I recall the butchers Rowbotham, Cooperative Society, Taylor and Kirk. Cooper's, oatcake makers in Arbourhay Street close to my Granny Talbot's home were also now conveniently placed to gain our patronage.

At the time of our move, my brothers Tony and Vincent were of an age to participate in part-time jobs and during the next two years each was employed either as paperboy by Mr and Mrs Jack Nield at the corner of Blagg Street, or as delivery boy by greengrocer Mr Jack Hopwood and his wife Hilda a few yards further up the road. They would retain a little of their earnings as spending money and began to bring home, on a regular basis, the tuppenny boys' paper publications of D C Thomson & Co, Dundee. Packed with good reading and well illustrated, these 'bloods' as we called them gave an added fillip to our lives. The Adventure was published Monday, the Wizard Wednesday, the Rover Thursday, the Hotspur Friday, and the Skipper on Saturday. This literary feast was augmented by the weekly delivery of my mother's Red Letter, also a Thomson publication which, although a women's paper, retained a strong family flavour.

The Premier Cinema, Vincent Street, had two pay boxes; one above the main steps and the other at the little window, right of centre, for the cheaper seats.

# Chapter Fifteen
## Entertainments

To a large extent, the contentment I experienced with Mr Tattersall continued when my fellow pupils and I moved up to Mr Ernest Baker's class 4 in 1937. For those of us destined for Central School - Vincent had already been there a year - this would be our final year at Daybrook.

Mr Baker, whom we referred to as 'Daddy' took a great deal of pride in his footwear and always wore highly polished, thick-soled boots. It was said of him (and was probably true) that whenever he bought a pair of boots he had them 'repaired' at once to bring the sole and heel thickness to his liking. He was good at adding polish to his pupils education as well, and embraced a broad spectrum of subjects. Strong emphasis was placed on literature. Many poems had to be learnt by heart. John Masefield's 'Sea Fever' and 'Cargoes' are still great favourites of mine. Longfellow's 'Hiawatha' had many an airing in our class and Aesop's Fables, Gulliver's Travels and The Wind in The Willows enriched our lives during that year.

Decorum was not a strong point with Mr Baker. Not only would he throw chalk at the inattentive in class, his wooden-backed duster was just as likely to be used as a missile and clouts from either hand were not uncommon. His heavy handedness was to cause ructions one Friday afternoon during an art period. We had been asked to bring a knife, fork and spoon from home to make pencil sketches of them in class. I was seated alongside Fred Slater who was relating some tale to me in a low voice and I was listening attentively as we worked, when suddenly a shadow fell upon us from behind. Glancing up and behind him, Fred spotted the heavy hand of Mr Baker poised above him and raised his own hand, which was holding his fork, to protect himself. The outcome was inevitable and a badly wounded Mr Baker lost his temper and poor Fred suffered greatly as a result. Naturally, the matter did not end there and it is likely Mr Baker improved his own education that afternoon for Fred could do no wrong from that point on.

On the whole, though, Daddy Baker had much on the credit side. He instilled in us pride in the British Empire - Robert Clive and the Indian Mutiny were pet themes - and he had total belief in the League of Nations. He was a good artist with sound creative ideas. I particularly enjoyed producing stippled stencil designs under his direction and, in a general sense, I believe he regarded me as one of his top boys. He organised a class library too, and encouraged us to take books home.

With the move to his class, swimming was added to the syllabus, with a period one afternoon each week, spent in the Public Baths in Davenport Street. On the day of our first planned visit to the baths we attended school with our bathing trunks and towel, as instructed. As afternoon schooling commenced Mr Baker made an appeal to us. Two lads from the upstairs classrooms were too poor to own bathers, he said. Nor had they the penny necessary to hire the briefs available at the baths. "Which two of you boys are willing to lend these lads their bathers?" he asked. There was no response. "Come on, you miserable lot," he admonished, "It's not much to ask." Still there was no response. Well, that did it. Mr B ranted and raged at us. He told us of all the years he'd been teaching, he'd never had such a rabble of selfish, uncaring, mean, ungenerous layabouts in all his life.

In the end, deeply disturbed by his contempt, I raised my hand and another lad followed suit shortly after. We handed our bathing trunks over with the understanding they would be returned to us as our two groups crossed on the journey to and from the baths. Of course when the bathers were returned to us they were wet. I dare say the two beneficiaries had had the presence of mind to put them through the little mangle the baths provided but they still held a lot of water and undressing and pulling on a wet pair of swimming trunks falls far short of being a blissful experience. What's more, having agreed to that first concession the practice of borrowing our two pairs of trunks was endorsed as a regular routine. Never have I felt so uncharitable about charity!

Going to the pictures in my boyhood years was an experience I never took for granted. Each visit was an exhilarating treat and on the odd occasion when a copy of Picturegoer magazine found its way to our house I would read it cover to cover. Hollywood was never far from my mind and many is the time I have imagined myself as a talented boy star with cameras trained upon me as I went about the business of day to day living.

My love for the medium was shared by most folk in those days. The cinema was 'escapism' and it was cheap. Throughout the first half of this century there wasn't an awful lot of 'brass' about in our town. Wages, generally, were low and yet the townsfolk enjoyed great wealth in the cinema sense. Apart from the Majestic - the youngest of them all, opening in 1922 - we had the Regal (1910), Picturedrome (1911), The New Cinema (1912) and the Premier (1919). Only the Majestic survives today. It is

REGAL Picture THEATRE TEL. 2449

DUKE STREET, MACCLESFIELD

HAS SECURED THE BIG FILM

CONTINUOUS DAILY FROM 6-30
(EXCEPT SATURDAY) TWO PERFORMANCES 6-30

Send your Children to the Saturda

● PICTURES TO SUIT THE CI

impossible to calculate the pleasure generated by just one of those establishments in its years of existence and no praise can be too high for any one of them.

The reader will know by now that my first allegiance was to the Cinema on Buxton Road but all were close to my heart and memories of boyhood days splay out like the spokes of a bicycle wheel. Saturday afternoon matinees were a wonderful film-going introduction for me. My first attendance at an evening performance was the Jubilee Year school treat to the Premier in 1935, a story I have already told. My second was an unexpected invitation to attend the Cinema during the time I was in Mr Baker's class. Good pal that he was it was no surprise for Hubert Glazebrook to call on us in Crew Avenue. He still lived in Waterloo Street across from my old home. This time he came with an invitation for me to join him and his mother at an evening performance at the Cinema. Permission from my mother was spontaneous and I agreed to meet them at the appointed time.

Our seats were in the 'posh' section of the theatre, two-thirds of the way up from the front in the centre section. The film was 'The Trail of the Lonesome Pine' starring youthful duo Henry Fonda and Fred MacMurray, Silvia Sidney and what pleased me most of all, Spanky McFarland, the tubby boy from the Our Gang series. This was the first outdoor film in the newly-perfected, three-colour Technicolor, which probably explains why we were there and the experience was definitely one for the memory locker.

Fate was to play its part, a year later, in enhancing my role as cinemagoer. My Granny Talbot of Arbourhay Street, although in fine physical condition, had become too absent-minded to live on her own and as her only daughter, Mother elected to look after her at our house. Gran was 68 at the time and despite her lapses of memory was able to do many little jobs in the home, not least of which was to churn out stockings for us boys at the drop of a ball of worsted in her lap.She used four steel needles and could 'turn a heel' with the best. Gran had always had a great love of the theatre ('thea-aiter', she pronounced the word) and despite her memory difficulties of present day things, retained a vast repertoire from days gone by. A happy soul, she would raise one hand sideways in an elegant pose, catch her skirt lightly with her other hand then, dancing gently, would sing:

"Georgie took me walking in the park;
In the park, for a lark.

The lovely summer breeze
Was blowing through the trees
When he carved my initials in the bark.
"Georgie made me sit upon his knees,
For a squeeze, 'neath the trees,
But my mother told me, never to sit me down,
But to keep on walking in the park!"

On other occasions she would remain in her chair by the fire and sing songs of great pathos. 'The Sailor's Grave', for example, was a mournful dirge guaranteed to soften the hardest heart. She had been born Ellen Houghton in 1869 and had lived in the Arbourhay Street area all her life. Her schooling had commenced at St Peter's, Windmill Street, where she paid tuppence fee to headmistress Miss Markland every Monday morning. From there she moved to Trinity Square School where Mr Armstrong was headmaster. Ellen had not been a strong child and when she was seventeen the family physician told her parents that only marriage could effect the desired change in her health! A year later she married James Murphy who some years earlier had left Dublin to join the Grenadier Guards and had seen service guarding the Queen at Windsor Castle. They were married at Hurdsfield Church by the Rev Laycock who, following the service, asked Jim why it was that he a catholic had agreed to be married at his church. "I left it entirely to her, sir," was the reply. Mr Laycock was suitably impressed.

The marriage produced two surviving infants, Jim, named after his father and Annie, born in 1895. Unfortunately, James the father died shortly after Annie's birth, reputedly from drinking cold lemonade on a hot day at Blackpool. Some years later, Ellen remarried becoming Mrs William Henry Clarke Talbot, which is as fine an English name I should think, as it is possible to have. Their three sons from this union were William, Ernest and Leslie. Their father died in 1933.

In planning a future life for Gran it was resolved that she be taken to the Cinema for each new programme. My brother Leslie would accompany her each Monday and I was chosen for the Thursday visit providing there had been a change in programme, which was usually the case. This duty - if you could call it that - was a tremendous fillip for me. Each Thursday evening I would be given a shilling by Mother, Gran would link my arm, and first stop would be the Rowbotham sisters' sweet shop close to their father's butcher's business on Hurdsfield Road. Always the order was the same; two ounce of Devon Cream toffee in one bag; one ounce of the same in another. This toffee at tuppence per quarter pound came in slabs and was packed in a tin depicting grazing cows. The slabs were segmented in such a way that if a hit with the little hammer broke the pieces accurately you received four perfectly square pieces in one ounce. This tasty offering, though, was usually so fresh and brittle it seldom shattered where intended and, anyway, I preferred it in a mixture of shapes. The two ounce square bag was for Gran and the cone-shaped one ounce bag was mine - Mother's ruling. The Cinema tickets were a fivepenny one for Gran and a half for me, and since the box-office didn't deal in ha'pennies I would hand over eight pence. Expenses for the evening's pleasure totalled ninepence ha'penny (slightly less than 4p in today's money) with tuppence ha'penny change for Mother. How about that for a bargain?

As if my cup wasn't near to overflowing already it was at this period that my parents chose to invest in our family's first wireless set. It was a Cossor model purchased from Lucking's in Sunderland Street and was powered by an accumulator, a popular wet-battery of the time. This could be 'charged' for sixpence either at Smith's Plumbing, Hurdsfield Road, or at Holland's hardware shop, Commercial Road. It was only when this valved model began operating that we all realised how much we had been missing. Now we had music, the news and weekly repetitive programmes we could anticipate and enjoy with much pleasure.

On Saturday evenings at 7.30 there was 'In Town Tonight' introduced by Eric Coates' 'Knightsbridge March'. London's traffic (the BBC sound-effects department demonstrated) was brought to a screeching halt for thirty minutes while the famous and the odd characters of life were interviewed. This was followed by Music Hall at 8 o'clock, and slotted in somewhere in the evening's entertainment was Robb Wilton as Mr Muddlecombe JP.

There was usually a classic serial on Sunday evenings and 'The Count of Monte Christo' for one, had us all on the edges of our seats. 'Monday Night at Seven', produced by Harry S Pepper and Douglas Moody, was a light-hearted mixture which included Inspector Hornleigh Investigates and Puzzle Corner compiled by Ronnie Waldman who, at a later date, married Rank star Lana Morris.

During the next year, on Wednesday evenings we had 'Band Waggon' with Arthur Askey and Richard (Stinker) Murdoch. The 'Waggon' was also the vehicle for rag and bone man Syd Walker who related a story each week ending with the question, "What would you do, chums?" No doubt many readers will have happy radio memories of those days also.

In the context of film-going, one chum was especially important to me in those late thirties. Bernard Ratcliffe lived in a little cottage sandwiched between the short run of shops in Commercial Road between Mrs Rutter, grocer, and Mr Bob Ashton, mixed sales. A most generous lad was Bernard. Each Saturday, at 12 noon, I would knock on his door and receive from him the current copy of the Dandy comic. How grateful I was for that service; but more than that, and more to the point, Bernard had access to the projection room at the Cinema. Whether he was employed there part-time or whether he enjoyed a certain freedom there, I cannot say, but he was a fount of information. He knew all about projection, changing reels, booking films, cost of rental and so on, and I relished this film showing insight.

## Chapter Sixteen
## Central School

The move to Central School in Byron Street had to be earned by examination during that year in Mr Baker's class, failing which Daybrook pupils climbed up the stone, spiral steps to Mr Cunningham's class upstairs and thence to Mr Brocklehurst's class until reaching the age of fourteen.

My move to Central School, which brought an end to free school dinners and clogged feet, meant that Vincent and I were together once again. My new school occupied the upper floor of the building with the girls' school below. It worked to a twin form system with forms 1 and 1A, 2 and 2A, 3 and 3A, with a merging to form 4 in the fourth year. The syllabus was the same for each class.

I got off to an encouraging start, being placed, with several of the lads from Daybrook in 1A, under the control of Mr Trickett, the language master. New classmate names included Frank Slack, Ken Slack and Willie Slack, none of them related, as far as I knew, Brian Hillman, who was history master Mr Rhodes' nephew, Philip Etchells, Gerald Rowley, Ernest MacDonald, Graham Naden, Kenneth Hilton, Jim Stacey, Bernard Cox, Cliff Bailey, Fred Holland,Tom Bailey, Hedley Preece, Walter Barratt, Brian Cooke, Brian Gee, Harold Tatton, Leslie Astbury, John Poolford and Geoff Langford. They were a class of young gentlemen, and that is not a cosmetic comment. Without exception they were friendly, good humoured and helpful towards each other and I cannot recall a single incident when tempers flared between any two.

From the start lunch periods posed a difficulty for me. Vincent had already spent two years at Central and was used to it, but at 12 noon we had to return across town to our home in Crew Avenue for dinner. Mother would clock-off from Tie Silks at 12.30, make her way home and prepare the meal. Granny Talbot would have often helped and peeled potatoes in the morning and had them nicely boiled by, say, 12.40, but in the next fifty minutes dinner had to be served and eaten, with Vincent and me back at Central. Had we had the necessary bus fare of one penny each there would have been no problem for a school bus service operated from Gladstone Square. As it was we had to run - Commercial Road, the Waters, Sunderland Street, Mill Lane and so on.

One would have thought that with this daily exercise, albeit on a full stomach, my little legs would have acquired running fitness, but my first experience of the Central cross-country run disproved that. We were not forewarned of the event. Suddenly, completely out of the blue, it was cross-country day and physical training that afternoon would take on a different guise. It was a daft thing to inflict on the boys without reasonable preparation and in my view did far more harm than good. I was perfectly happy about it at the time for I have always welcomed a challenge, and I entered into the spirit of the race whole-heartedly. We raced down Byron Street and crossed into Byron's Lane. I have always thought there is something magical about Byron's Lane. Even at walking pace the change from urban to rural within a matter of a minute or two is quite remarkable. On this day, though, I had competition more on my mind than pastoral beauty. The easy climb up Bullock's Lane brought us to the canal and its tow-path and the stench from the bone works assailed our nostrils as my legs slowed achingly and one lad after another passed me. The long run down London Road remains a painful memory.

It was a dismal performance and when I eventually arrived back at the school gate my position in the race was given as '28 low'. Just how many high places were credited before the low count commenced I never did learn, but I had done my best and resolved to do better next time. Just for the record, a year later I gained second place, a few yards behind Jim Stacey, so I did redeem myself.

This first taste of athletics had left me jiggered and my legs ached so much I made the mistake of retiring to my bed early that evening with the result that the next day I had stiffened so much I could scarcely walk. My hardy brother Vincent went off to school ahead of me that day and as I hobbled along Sunderland Street, my form master, Mr Trickett came abreast of me, having just alighted from his train at Central Station, and said, "Take your time, Hunter. I'll mark you in 'early' this morning, whatever time you get there." Crumbs of compassion, I already knew, were extremely rare at Central and I was grateful for this generous helping.

Strange to relate, as fond as I was of Mr Trickett during my stay at Central, it was he who penalised me with the only two stripes I received, for talking in class. The system of awarding stars and stripes as a means of commendation and punishment, respectively, left much to be desired. The very term seemed to imply a balanced formula and had it been so in practice the system would have been sound. It was far from being that. A star was difficult to acquire. It was composed of four quarters, each comprising six facets. For facet read 'G' for good. When a boy had achieved six G's in an exercise book, that is to say, in any one subject, he could apply to that subject's master for a quarter star, a pink form with space for four quarter-star insertions. To gain a full star he would need to excel in his work twenty-four times. On the other hand one could be awarded a stripe for the least bit of a thing, usually for being heard muttering to a class-mate. Whether or not a stripe was actually intended to cancel out a star I cannot be sure but the implication was there and that is the way I looked at it and why I say that, psychologically, the system was unsound and was a total negation of the desire to promote incentive and nurture encouragement.

Our headmaster, Robert Ethelred Houseman, MA, had come to Macclesfield from Croydon in 1935 to replace the departing Mr Barry. Small in stature with a small clipped moustache, Mr Houseman arrived at school each day in his Baby Austin (registration ETU 94) and would park it with its front bumper against the railings on the left of the bicycle shed. Once in the school he would don his black gown, of which he was justly proud, and whenever he needed to walk would do so at a brisk pace, his gown rustling behind him, riding on the disturbed air in his wake. He controlled the school bell which rested on a desk set on a dais at the front of the main hall. He would ring to announce morning assembly shortly after 9am and conduct the proceedings. Following assembly he would ring the bell at intervals throughout the day to indicate change of lessons. There were other times, not frequently, thank goodness, when the bell would ring between classes, indicating a special assembly; the bell had an ominous ring to it then, for punishment of someone was indicated.

Mr Houseman was a strict disciplinarian. Totally devoid of any sense of humour, he was quick to eradicate any manifestation of high jinks, and like Mr Brocklehurst in 'Jane Eyre' he had a penchant for making a spectacle of punishment. I was thoroughly sickened by one - what we termed - 'public flogging', where a certain boy had expressed his sense of humour over-exuberantly. A decent lad, he was verbally humiliated in front of the whole school before being called to the front for punishment. He was caned twice on each hand and then told to go in search of a chair and to bring it back with him. When the lad returned with the chair he had to lie across it while his buttocks were beaten. I likened the search for a chair to a condemned man being sent in search of the rope which was to hang him. Shocking! Not for Mr Houseman, a fatherly word to an errant boy in his study, or private and fair physical punishment on the hand when merited.

Few would have had any objection to that in those days.

It is my view that Mr Houseman was an anachronism, given the quality of pupil attending Central at that time. It may well be that many people in certain areas of our society today would welcome his like to redress the balance in the decline of behaviour since those days. One audacious prankster, more mirthful than malicious, I suspect, placed a six-inch nail at an angle behind one of the headmaster's car tyres one morning and since the vehicle had first to be reversed for departure, a motive appeared obvious. This act added a piquancy to the pupils' mid-morning breather that day and when a first-former admitted to having returned inside the school to report the misdemeanour my brother Vincent made the mistake of facetiously suggesting to the boy he would be better employed minding his own business.

This remark, ostensibly incriminating as it was, was reported to Mr Houseman with the result that Vincent was questioned by the Head in his study. The headmaster was convinced he had found the culprit but Vincent strongly denied the insinuation. Yes, he admitted, he had made the unchivalrous remark but knew nothing of the prank itself, and Mr Houseman was frustrated by his stance. "The place for you," he said, "is in a reformatory! Get back to your class."

That evening Vincent reported the whole story to Dad, who bristled when he heard the final comment. He wrote a letter to Mr Houseman deploring the remark made to Vincent and suggested that the Head, in his turn, was unfit to be in charge of a boys' school and would be better employed running a Nazi concentration camp!

On receipt of this letter, Mr Houseman said to Vincent, "You can inform your father I will be happy to discuss things with him providing he can conduct himself in a proper manner." So Dad went to the school and had a private meeting with the Head in his study. Later, Vincent was sent for and Dad said to him, "Vincent, I'm going to ask you one question and I want the absolute truth from you. Did you or did you not place that nail under Mr Houseman's car tyre?" Vincent replied, "No, I did not, Dad."

Turning to the headmaster, my father said, "My son's word is good enough for me and I am asking you to accept it as well." "I do accept, now, that that is the truth of the matter," responded Mr Houseman.

Before leaving the school that day my father warned Mr Houseman against any future victimisation of his two sons. Whether this warning would be heeded remained to be seen.

**Hurdsfield Road/Gladstone Square: The newsagents on the right belonged to the Nield family throughout the century until after World War II.**

## Chapter Seventeen
## Grocer's boy

During that year of 1938 Tony and Vincent had been happily engaged in their part-time jobs. Tony delivered papers, morning and evening for John Willie Nield and Vincent was grocer's delivery boy for the Hopwoods, both shops being within yards of each other on Hurdsfield Road. Then the Hopwoods decided to move to pursue a similar venture in Chester Road and they sold the Hurdsfield shop to Mrs Florrie Wright who had no previous experience of the retail trade. As was customary and sensible, Mrs Wright and the Hopwoods ran the shop together for a short period as part of the transaction and Mrs Wright developed a great fondness for Vincent. She was saddened when he elected to move to Chester Road with the Hopwoods following the changeover. At this point I stepped into the breach to save the day. I was just eleven years old and it was my first part-time job.

Mrs Wright was a lovely lady. She was of the Avery family of Langley and previously had been widowed a young Mrs Birchenough with a young son, Joe. Tragedy had followed tragedy and later she had lost the young, angelic Joe as well but her faith had stood her in good stead. Her second husband, George, was employed on the bins by Macclesfield Corporation. He tended to be rather reserved, probably due to a sight weakness, for his spectacles had very thick lenses and I likened them - without humour, you understand - to bottle bottoms. In the course of time I found him to be just as kind and gentle as his wife who, incidentally, was assisted in the shop by her sister Miss Elsie Avery who came regularly from Langley.

Precisely what my duties were supposed to be from the outset or what wages I received does not readily come to mind. For one thing I seemed to become a member of the family immediately and although Fridays after school and all day Saturday duties were obligatory, I would pop in after school on other days and assist on a regular basis. Remuneration was not a big issue either since I was totally devoid of mercenary intent and happily handed over to my mother whatever coinage came my way, probably in the region of two shillings and sixpence per week.

As shops go, Mrs Wright's was quite sizeable. The floor was slightly higher than the outside pavement so the doorway had a step and the shop counter was on the right as one entered, running at a right angle to the road. Behind the door there were two or three feet of space to the back wall. A deep shelf, partitioned into sections and at adult waist height sloped gently forward on stout wooden legs and contained the bulk of the fruit for sale. Underneath, light from the glass panelled door fell upon a crate of sterilised milk and a large set of see-saw scales with a generous scoop dish and a supporting cast of weights. Two substantial wooden potato containers which tapered downwards to the stone-flagged floor came next followed by various open boxes and open-necked sacks. These, containing mainly

vegetables, jostled for space to catch the eye.

One tastefully lined box would contain fresh diced vegetables, the price-ticket describing the assortment as 'pot herbs', an ideal mixture for soups and stews. Finally, tucked away in the far corner close by the door leading to the back of the shop were a case or two of the new household bleach, 'Lanry', a name coined from the christian names of the producers, Alan and Harry Brown. Above this array were shelves containing tinned foods and dried goods to which customers could help themselves and bring to the counter.

Given decent weather (and we seemed to get more of it in those days), goods would be displayed outside the shop. It was not unusual for such shops to have a narrow board hinged to the window-sill with a supporting chain at each end which could be lowered to form a shelf for this purpose. Cabbage, cauliflower etc, and punnets of strawberries in the summer would advertise themselves in this way.

As a Central schoolboy, I owed much to the influence of Art master Mr Brocklehurst. His was one of the few classes in which I showed any aptitude. My talent was quickly utilized by Mrs Wright and to my duties was added that of ticket-writer. I was into 'shadow writing' in those days (my own description), which was a fragmented and illusory form of writing which fascinated my employer and undoubtedly elevated me in her estimation.

Pricing of goods had to be calculated and monitored carefully, for 15 yards up the road Mr and Mrs Fred Worth had a similar business. A ticket ploy failed to work for us on one occasion. Following instructions, I produced a potato ticket which read 'King Edward's 7lbs for 6d'. No sooner was the ticket in place when into the shop came an eagle-eyed middle-aged woman. Glancing critically at my most recent art creation, she commented, "King Edward's, seven pounds for sixpence? I'm not paying that. I can get 'em at Fred Worth's for a penny a pound!" And out of the shop she stormed.

Mid-week I was always available for the weighing of produce and the spontaneous delivery of orders. "Would you like the boy to deliver them to you?" was a question often asked of customers, but my Friday and Saturday duties were more premeditated. On Fridays, after school, I would collect my note-book from the shop and stroll leisurely around the area collecting orders for delivery the next day. I was glad to be introduced to the job during a period of light nights for one of my calls was to the vicarage adjoining Hurdsfield Church. The Rev Isaac Hutchinson's home was, like the church, old and set well back from the road and I had to flirt briefly with the grave-stones to reach it. I think a dark baptism to that duty would have scared the life out of me!

Come Saturday I would bring out the cart from the back of the shop - a shallow wooden box with a pair of push-chair wheels and shaft handles - and delivery would commence.

My first delivery of an order to Mrs Hutchinson at Hurdsfield Vicarage has stayed in my memory ever since. Having paid me the required sum for her order Mrs H proffered a penny tip. No, thank you very much, I said. She was clearly surprised and puzzled by my refusal and tried again, but I was adamant. I could not bring myself to explain that I regarded her money as holy - God's money, in fact - and I was unworthy of it. From that point until my delivery the next week this lady must have given the matter much thought for having paid for her second order she produced a money-box.

"Would you like to take this home with you?" she asked. "It's a Church Missionary box and at any time you have a copper to spare you can put it in the box, and in due course it will do a lot of good. Here, there's a penny tip for you to start the ball rolling ...." and she dropped the coin through the slot and each week afterwards would tip me with a penny and say "....and that's for your box." What a clever and perceptive lady she was! The box was given a set spot on the sideboard at home for use by all the family and was returned filled at a later date.

Of course I still remember many of the families I visited, even though it is almost sixty years ago. A Saturday morning call would be to the Kay residence, the first house on the left in Fence Avenue. Mr Kay had a business at Lower Heys. His wife was a staunch supporter of the Girl Guide and Brownie movement and they had a son, Stanley and a daughter, June. I called also at the Francis home in Brocklehurst Avenue, opposite Hurdsfield House. Mr Francis was chemistry master at my school and he and his wife had two daughters, the youngest of whom, Margaret, developed into a superb athlete and became British Sprint Champion and a top international before becoming a doctor.

The Gortons in Queens Avenue were also on my round as were the Clarkes a little further along on the other side. Mr Gorton was a renowned french-polisher. His wife was a petite and most attractive lady. They had young lads, Alan and Stanley and little daughter, Marjorie, who today lives at Weston, Stafford. The Clarkes, I believe I am right in saying, had close connections with the Royal Oak public house which stood back from the road in Gladstone Square.

In Hawthorn Way I recall the Potts family on the left as the road came to an end. Their two little girls were like fairy tale princesses and, young lad though I was, I also took note of the dark, mature beauty of Olga of the Compton (or was it Compston?) family when I called on them in the crescent of Nicholson Avenue as it swept round the top before descending hurriedly to form the junction with Brocklehurst Avenue. Yes, indeed, I remember them all so well .....

Sadly, Mrs Wright never savoured at the shop the contentment she had sought and after I had been with her for about two years she decided to call it a day and retire gracefully with George to their cottage higher up

Hurdsfield Road. Her shop became Ferris's shoe repairers. Her retirement meant a door had closed for me also but, as is often the case, another door opened for me shortly afterwards.

W. Garfield Weston, Member of Parliament for Macclesfield through World War II. A Canadian, he was a highly successful businessman who donated vast sums to our fight against Germany. He also gave greatly of his time and money to youth projects in Macclesfield both during and after the War.

## Chapter Eighteen
## Macclesfield Times 1939

As my story moves into 1939, I have been tempted to take a look through the pages of the Macclesfield Times of that momentous year for anything that catches my eye. The Children's Circle, presented by Auntie Hilda, was a column never missed by me since I learned to read. This feature included a weekly birthday list and in the first three months of 1939 the published names of boys and girls I knew personally, or would come to know, should generate interest among many readers of this book.

| | | | |
|---|---|---|---|
| Jessie Dutton, | 12th Jan | Philip Barber, | 21st Feb |
| Vernon F Connor, | 16th Jan | Betty Biddulph, | 22nd Feb |
| Sheila Torson, | 17th Jan | Dorothy Booth, | 6th Feb |
| Alan M Parramore, | 22nd Jan | Douglas Boulton, | 28th Feb |
| Cecilia Osbaldeston, | 22nd Jan | Brian Surtees, | 1st March |
| Joyce Cork, | 23rd Jan | Grant Turner, | 17th March |
| Norman McGuinness, | 14th Feb | Doreen May Wright, | 27th March |
| Thomas Hassal, | 19th Feb | Joan Kirk, | 1st April |

Here are other interesting news items from that year:

**Jan 6** - Having won the amateur talent competition which was held at the Majestic Picture House last week, Master Neville Thomas, boy singer of Macclesfield, will consequently make a broadcast from Radio Lyons. Miss Alice Swindells, the well-known local piano-accordionist was second. There were 74 entries.

**Jan 20** - Police promotions: Detective Sergeant F H Dent has been promoted to the rank of Inspector and Detective Constable Fearick is appointed Detective Sergeant.

**Jan 27** - The Mayor, Ald H E Mowbray, appealed to the citizens of Macclesfield to respond to the call for enrolment of volunteers under the National Service Scheme.

**Feb 3** - The King's School players presented 'The Amazing Dr Clitterhouse' and the Hovis Amateur Players offered 'The Rotters' in the Parochial Hall, Roe Street.

**Feb 10** - Cheap LMS trips from Macclesfield to Birmingham - two shillings and fivepence return. London - nine shillings return.

**Feb 14** - The Chief Constable (Mr H Sheasby) was decorated by the King at Buckingham Palace with the King's Police Medal.

**Feb 14** - There was a steady increase in the number of persons volunteering for

ARP work in Macclesfield.

**March 3** - The Macclesfield ARP department appeals for volunteer cardboard carton assemblers into which inhabitants of the borough will place their gas masks.

**March 27** - Gas masks and cartons distributed in Higher Hurdsfield and Rainow.

**April 6** - Auntie Hilda thanks Harold, Arthur and Philip Genders for the silver paper.

**April 14** - The 7th Cheshire Regiment has been congratulated by the Secretary of State for War, Mr Leslie Hore Belisha on the success of its recruiting campaign to reach war establishment.

**April 21** - Macclesfield Infirmary's new Nurses Home was opened two days ago, by Mr JF Morton, managing director of Hovis Ltd. Built by Cooper Bros., the project is still £1,400 short of achieving 'free of debt' status. The timing of the ceremony coincides with Mr Morton's completion of 50 years service with Hovis. It is intended to recognise Mr Morton's jubilee of service by providing a new recreational hall for the Macclesfield employees at a cost of £4,500.

**April 28** - The Town's new Catholic Church, St Edward's, London Road, was consecrated by the Bishop of Shrewsbury.

- The Chief Constable (Mr H Sheasby) appeals for more volunteers (ARP) "in view of the urgency of the situation".

**May 12** - LMS bookings for Barnaby Holidays. Blackpool, period return, ten shillings.

- A 'blackout' and air raid exercise will take place on Wednesday, 17th May, between 12-30am and 2pm.

- The Repertory Theatre is to close down on Saturday, May 13th, due to lack of support. Housed in the Brocklehurst Memorial Hall it has been the town's only live theatre since the Opera House was burnt to the ground on April 4th, 1931.

**May 19** - This paper is happy to state that there is no truth in the rumour, current in the town, that Dr H Jaffe, of Cumberland Street, has dropped dead in his car.

**June 2** - North Western Road Car Company. Cheap evening excursion to Buxton, Sunday, June 4th. One shilling.

- New Austin Van at WH Hyde Ltd Hobson Street/Vincent Street. Price £120.

**July 7** - Miss Madeline Gibson, a teacher at Trinity Square School, fourth daughter of Mr and Mrs J E Gibson, 'Pen Dinas', Giant's Wood Lane, Congleton, was married to Mr Stanley Alwyn Bevan, son of Mr and Mrs M A Bevan, Park View, Congleton, at St Michael's Church, Hulme Walfield, on Wednesday. The bridegroom is Registrar of births, deaths and marriages at Congleton, whilst his father holds a similar position at Macclesfield.

**Aug 11** - The intimation by Mr J R Remer, Conservative MP for Macclesfield since 1918 that he does not intend to seek re-election to Parliament created much surprise. He introduced to the Advisory Committee, as a likely successor, Mr W

Garfield Weston, of Marlow, Bucks.

**Aug 25** - Tills, Stationers, 1 Samuel Street, can now offer black-out paper and sealing tape for sale.

- Broadbents 46 Mill Street have black blind cloth from ninepence per yard.

- Mr Garfield Weston chosen as a prospective Conservative candidate.

**Sept 3** - War declared. Town's cinemas close for one week.

**Sept 7** - Government rules that cinemas, on re-opening, must close at 10pm.

- The Macclesfield Times to be published Thursdays instead of Fridays.

**Oct 12** - Mr Garfield Weston 'adopted' by Macclesfield Conservatives.

**Nov 9** - Ration books (60,000) now being issued.

- A series of summonses have been served for showing lights in the black-out. A claim that the police officer and ARP warden must have seen the moon's reflection in a bathroom window was rejected and the offender fined five shillings.

**Nov 30** - ARP sirens to be tested.

The reference to Inspector Dent's promotion in those snippets reminded me of how fine and dignified a man he was as he returned from duty each day walking with measured pace up Hurdsfield Road to his home on The Crescent. There was some 'distance' between us in those days, I being only 11 or 12 years old, but in later years we were drawn together by a mutual love of literary competitions and remained good friends into his retirement and up to his death. There was a further strong police influence in my area then for in Brocklehurst Avenue - yards from my home in Crew Avenue - lived Constables Bailey, Greenall and Johnson, all family men, each meriting the high degree of respect accorded to 'beat' men of those times.

I could not resist including the marriage report of my much loved Trinity Square school teacher, Miss Gibson. Many years later, when I had a family of my own I met Mrs Bevan, in her retirement. Her husband had passed away some months earlier and she was finding it difficult to come to terms with his loss, but I was gratified to discern from her sadness that theirs had been a supremely happy union. At that same meeting she delighted me with the disclosure that a drawing of my younger brother Leslie, which I had produced in her class, had remained one of her proudest possessions; a tribute for me to savour.

A young John Hedley Palin poses outside the Commercial Road grocer/butchers shop he managed for the family concern before World War II. Company reps especially appreciated the hospitality on offer when they called.

### Chapter Nineteen
### Cakes and canings

By this time we Hunters had woven ourselves comfortably into our new communal life. We had established a great fondness for the Henshalls at number one whose daughter May had taken a strong liking to my young sister Dorothy. For reasons I cannot explain, when I think of these two together - the beautiful blonde young lady and the little eight year old lass, a song which must have been meaningful to them at the time, comes to mind. It went:

> Little old lady, passing by,
> Catching everyone's eye;
> She has such a charming manner,
> Sweet and shy.

It was soon after this time that May Henshall was courted by a young and handsome Gawsworth chap, Gerald Hague, and in due course they were married. May's brother, Harry, married Miss May Belfield at a later date.

My pal, Alec Houghton at number five had left school and begun employment with master baker Mr Roland Coppenhall of Black Road, and consequently from that point on I didn't see as much of Alec as I would have wished. The Coppenhall bakehouse, I recall, was an incongruous stone structure rather like a rude Hebridean crofter's cottage which had been deposited at the roadside by a cyclone in Wizard of Oz manner. Another curiosity close by was a tree growing out of the tall chimney of an old sawmill.

The main event for my family that year came as a complete surprise to Vincent and me one day early in May when we returned home from school. Our mood was buoyant, for the May Fair was assembled in Waters Green as we passed through and there was a promise of excitement in the air. The real excitement awaited us at home that very day when Dad announced that our family had increased with the birth to Mother of a further son. We were aware of our mother going into St Mary's Hospital, Manchester, for 'something' but we hadn't expected this and it all took some getting used to.

Well, Mother came home quite soon with little Terry. What a welcome the little chap received! We were all so attentive; he couldn't feed, he couldn't be 'changed', without an audience and there was no shortage of arms to cradle him in loving embrace. It was natural that I should feel a special bond with the lad but the passing of time and a mutual love of sport was to ensure our bond would remain strong and sustained throughout the years.

Shops in the Hurdsfield Road/Commercial Road stretch which had a particular influence on our life then are worthy of mention. Miss Rebecca Moores' sweet shop on the corner of Adelaide Street always had a good display of Needler's chocolates in the window, all at fourpence per quarter pound. Placed symmetrically in the centre of her display were two exotically-shaped bottles containing tiny cachous to sweeten the breath, sold at fourpence per half ounce. The name of the blue variety does not come to mind but the pink cachous were called Phul Nana. I tasted one once and considered it no different to a Dolly Mixture which could be bought at one-sixteenth of the price!

A peculiarity of Miss Moore's shop was that a wall of empty sweet bottles concealed customers' view of her scales. I would have thought this practice was unlawful but she persisted with it. I don't doubt for one moment that customers were ever denied their true measure but I suspect her fastidious attention to weight detail ensured no customer received a Phul Nana cachou as a bonus! Diagonally across the road on the bottom corner of Smyth Street was Pierce's chip shop which played an admirable role on some days each week providing us with a speedy lunch.

Slightly lower down the road was Mr Fred Drinkwater's premises known as The Little Favourite Shop. He was a grocer and corn merchant. A likeable chatty chap, he seemed always to be sucking a morsel of cheese. He had two grown-up sons, Harry and Fred, who appeared to be twins. Fred junior was employed by Hollands', the ironmonger's shop in Commercial Road where folk could take their wireless accumulator to be re-charged for sixpence. On fine days young Fred would bring merchandise out from the shop on to the pavement: lawn mowers, trellis fencing and a good range of gardening tools. This display added a touch of character to the area and nobody complained of obstruction.

Our new butcher was Mr Rowbotham whose shop faced the Steeple Street opening. His two daughters had kept the sweet shop a few yards lower down, for some years and one of them, Mary, was to marry Mr Reg Spearing round about that time. A special sweet treat on sale at this shop was buttermilk toffee, a light caramel which, like Devon Cream Toffee, came in slabs and was broken by light taps with a little hammer.

I am unsure at what time Stubb's cake shop on the bottom corner of Blagg Street became Heath's Cafe, but once Heath's took over it developed into a thriving eating establishment. One could wield a knife and fork inside or take a basin for meat, veg and gravy consumption at home. They were bakers and confectioners as well and we regularly purchased what my mother described as 'Ginny Lynn's'; large, flat, fruit scones you could slice carefully, horizontally, and butter on the inside or like us, simply apply butter on the top.

Barber Jess Taylor, whose shop was a few yards on, was reminiscent of Fleet Street's infamous Sweeney Todd, in that once he had you in his chair he would be sure to 'polish you off' in double quick time. Not in a lethal sense, of course, but he had earned the sobriquet 'the lightening barber'. On the wall above his two wash-basins was a framed pencil sketch of a Wyandotte hen. New customers would ask about this drawing - it was facing them as they sat in the 'business' chair - and Jess delighted in telling the story of how, as a lad, he was awarded first prize for this sketch by a certain body of judges who complimented him on his poultry anatomy accuracy. If he had copied this bird from a cigarette card illustration, as I suspect, it was a fine achievement for it was a sizeable effort and admirably proportioned.

Within yards was the Co-op which had two counters that ran at right-angles to the road. We continued to get our bread and best butter from the Co-op and still chanted "3-0-9-8" when asked for our 'divi' number as if it were some magical incantation.

Mrs Chatfield's hardware shop came just after the space where the Royal Oak pub went back from the road. Paraffin, pots and pans, crockery, rolls of linoleum, etc, this shop was a veritable Aladdin's cave of homely usefulness and it is likely our zinc bath in Waterloo Street came from there. Mrs Chatfield's daughter Alice, was married to Macclesfield Corporation stonemason, Jack Cobham, a fine, upright man in every sense. The Cobham's, two boys and two girls of Eastgate, had known hard times. Orphaned in the early 1920s, their Uncle Bill (Mr Garlick, the firm-but-fair Cinema minder) had helped raise them until Jack reached an age to become main bread-winner.

A grocer, baker and confectioner's shop meriting the highest praise was Palin's next to the Woodman Inn on the corner of Norton Street. Palin's cakes were very special. There were custard tarts, fruit tarts, vanilla cuts and coffee cream slices, all at tuppence each, and a variety of modest offerings at a penny. Meat pies were a celebrated line also. I was sent on an errand to Palin's one lunch-time and found just one man customer ahead of me. Young Hedley Palin, impeccably dressed in his whites, asked me to be patient. The gentleman on my side of the counter was a 'traveller' and Hedley was just fixing him up with some lunch. Two flour cakes had already been sliced open and Hedley proceeded to butter them, stroking a huge mound of best butter with his knife, which struck me as being rather comical. Then came the ham, carved thick off the bone with mustard to follow. What a feast the man would have - what I saw that day was probably a regular routine.

And finally, it's cakes again. This time the Steam Bakery on the corner of Queen Street where Mr and Mrs Leah had baked their way into folklore. Their speciality was cream scones; plate size rounds with a cross indentation for quarter separation, filled with cream and jam and covered with 'Swiss' icing on top. Fourpence, these were, for a full round. The Leah's also made succulent jam-filled crisp biscuits and assorted fruit pies baked in traditional meat pie tins. You would probably have paid thruppence for those. The stock brick by the right side of their door bore a faded legend in white paint which read: 'Ice Cream Pies', obviously a delicacy on offer before my time. Faded paint could also be seen across from Leah's shop, high on the gable end of Wainwright's leather factory at the end of Thorp Street, known as 'Clock Alley' in the old days. Intended to catch the eye of train travellers in the late 19th century, it read, Mother Shipton's Soap, and the lady herself, wearing her tall, black hat, was faintly visible as well.

It is terribly sad that I should look back on my three years at Central School with such distaste for, overall, the school had much to commend it. The form masters were of a high qualify but had varying temperaments. I regarded Mr Francis (Science), Mr Blackford (English), Mr Brocklehurst (Art), Mr Rhodes (History), and Mr Coups (Woodwork) as comfortably placid types who seldom allowed their tempers to rise. Mr Kirk (Geometry) with a bark much worse than his bite could be very explosive, and how his desk-top stood up to the harsh treatment of being raised and crashed down so often is beyond me. He consistently frightened me but seldom issued a stripe. Mr Trickett (Languages), who it was rumoured, did not see eye-to-eye with headmaster, Mr Houseman, could be intolerant, as the two stripes he gave me indicate, but he was a popular master and contrived to ensure his pupils gained an unusually high mark in examinations. This could not be said of Mr Jackson (Geography) who possessed the only rotating board - green, not black - in the school. Whether by accident or design, Mr Jackson tended to include, in his examination test papers, items not previously covered in the syllabus. The result was low markings.

Art periods with Mr Brocklehurst and English with Mr Blackford gave me most pleasure and most marks in exams. I regarded these subjects as recreational. Conversely, my vain attempts to understand Geometry must have had Euclid spinning in his grave. Mr Brocklehurst's art tuition was almost exclusively of an indoor variety. He would talk of outside water-colour painting and advise on materials but we never actually went outside as a group for art periods. We concentrated on poster-painting and manuscript writing and would make perspective drawings of churches out of our heads. He knew his stuff did Daddy Brock and although I did not realise it at the time it was he, principally, who paved the way for my satisfying and challenging working life.

The sporting competition between the school 'houses', Drake, Hood, Hawke and Nelson gave a fillip to life and the joy was exquisite when I was decked out in my Hood football strip. I enjoyed being a member of the school choir under the tutelage of Mr Coups and competed in several musical festivals. One woodwork project my form tackled with zest was the making of bamboo flutes. Gerald Rowley's father had some standing at Ray's Mineral Water Works and supplied the cork stoppers for the mouthpieces. That flute of mine was probably the best piece of work I did at Central for having bored the finger holes, Mr Coups declared the instrument precisely in tune and required no subtle adjustment.

But over all this pleasantry, Mr Houseman's influence hung like a pall. The day Vincent and I were caned in the hall before the whole school has remained a bitter memory. I suppose I am just as likely as anyone to subconsciously sanitize a past embarrassment but I do not believe that is true in this case. Vincent and I have always believed we were the victims of injustice and reprisal that day. The prelude to punishment followed the normal format. The assembly bell rang its ominous peal, classrooms emptied and the school hall filled. Mr Houseman gave the customary lecture on the virtue that had been violated. On this occasion no name was mentioned until the end of his address.

The Head's theme soon became apparent. It was his job to instill self-discipline in his pupils; procrastination was the thief of time; promptness was a most worthy attribute in life, etc, etc. Any unease I felt dissipated. Punctuality was for me, I reckoned, a safe category. Even when he finally mentioned "two brothers", I was unconcerned, and pondered which two brothers, poor devils, could he be alluding to? Then came the bombshell: "Will the two Hunter brothers come to the front of the hall!" Vincent was some way behind me with the senior boys so there was no chance to confer and we made our separate ways to the front where Mr Houseman spaced us apart to allow for the sideways spread of arms when caning took place.

Vincent was made of sterner stuff than me and appealed for justice and fair play. Ignoring this, Mr Houseman flexed his rod between his hands and told him, "Since you are the eldest I intend to treat you more severely." At that, Vincent glanced sideways at me and in that hushed hall his voice must have carried to all parts. "Geoffrey," he said, "You are not to cry for this man." Naturally, I shared his resolve to limit the headmaster's satisfaction. Vincent was given two strokes of the cane on each hand and I received half that punishment. We agreed not to tell our father. Vincent was too near his fourteenth birthday to stir things up. "I will be leaving Central soon," he said. "Chances are things will be easier for you when I've gone." Late in 1939 he took his leave, a year earlier than was officially allowed.

It has always been Vincent's view that an over-zealous prefect was responsible for our punishment that day. On duty at the top of the stairs following lunch he had spotted us on several occasions in the last seconds dashing like mad up the stairs in the wake of the main body of pupils and had reported our lack of decorum to the headmaster.

It was about that time that Mother returned to her silk weaving duties and to me fell the pleasant task of delivering six month old Terry in his pram to Glegg Street nursery each morning on my way to Central and collecting him after school in the afternoon. I used the old Trinity route each time so that twice daily I crossed my beloved Waterloo Street at the Dicken Street/Davies Street junction. These spells of togetherness with the lad were sweet phases in my life then and I arrived at school in a more contented frame of mind.

## Chapter Twenty
## The year before the War

1939 was an important year for me, being the first full year of my emancipation in the cinema sense. Children's matinees were no longer for me. Thanks to the joyful duties escorting Granny Talbot to the pictures most Thursday evenings the adult cinema had now drawn me exclusively into its embrace and I was happy to succumb to its assorted charms.

Politically, there was tension and our country entered that year with a sense of foreboding. Just three months earlier our Prime Minister, Mr Chamberlain's assurance of "Peace in our time" on his return from Munich had been accepted with relief and belief by some, and as a transitory truth by others; but whether there was a spluttering fuse or not, life had to go on, and for me that meant continued unhappiness at school on the one hand and my preference to be 'educated' in a darkened auditorium on the other, whenever funds would allow.

I was eleven years old now and I got off to a very quick start that new year with a matinee showing of 'Spawn of the North' at the Cinema on Monday, January 2nd. This Canadian fishing story starred George Raft, Henry Fonda, and a surprising, but shrewdly cast Dorothy Lamour. Icebergs added greatly to the film's visual appeal. An old work's pal, Raymond Frost, remembers that particular time also. Raymond lived in Byron Street in those days and recalls obtaining a ticket, courtesy of the Macclesfield, Bollington and District Children's Help Society, to attend a free matinee at the Regal Picture House on Wednesday, January 4. Before the show commenced, Mr S Cass, proprietor of the Regal - as usual, wearing plus-fours - faced his eager audience and said, "Well, boys and girls, we have two films for you today. The first is a picture of the famous radio programme 'In Town Tonight', and the other is a Western starring one of your favourites, Tim McCoy."

Mr Cass made no charge to the Society for film or theatre hire. Members of the Society were present and following the performance each youngster was given a bag containing an apple, an orange, and sweets. I am grateful to Raymond for that story. A keen cinemagoer to this day, he has attended Macclesfield's Majestic cinema on a regular weekly basis for forty years.

I have my own little story of the Cass family generosity, but it is a

127

story that has to be told out of sequence of my main narrative theme for it occurred ten years after World War II ended. In the mid-fifties I lived in Cotton Street behind the Regal Picture House. My son Paul was a two-year-old and on his early evening walks, prior to his bedtime, we would call at the Regal about 7.30 for a chat with Mrs Cass at her pay-box in the sloped open-ended entrance to her cinema. Paul loved to be lifted up to see and to chat with 'the lady in the window' and he and Mrs Cass developed a great affection for each other.

One evening while thus engaged there was a movement to my left and a glance confirmed that an elderly man had entered the enclosed area from the street. Instinctively, I backed away from the window, Paul in my arms, to allow the newcomer to purchase his ticket. Unexpectedly, the man bent down into a crouched position and shuffled behind me as fast as his old legs would permit, before passing through the swing doors into the cinema.

A smiling Mrs Cass, who had seen everything, responded to the puzzlement in my face. "Just a poor pensioner," she explained. "He's been coming here for quite some time now. Never misses a programme and always comes halfway through the first house. He brings a bit of a tea card or cigarette packet cut to shape. The usherette is instructed to accept his token without comment and to treat it in the normal way. She returns half of it to him and shows him to his seat. It would be cruel to spoil his bit of pleasure, wouldn't it?"

I am sure readers will agree that a heartening little tale like that makes for better reading than 'politically correct' decisions which have soured the news in more recent times.

During the second week of 1939 the Cinema presented 'Rosalie' with Nelson Eddy and Eleanor Powell, on the first three nights only. At that time these names meant little to me, nor was the title one that would normally have attracted me, but I was collecting a film star series of cigarette cards at that period and Mr Eddy was already in my pack. His birthday, as stated on the back of his card, was the same as my own (given that there was a 27 year difference) and from somewhere I managed to rustle up the required thruppence to see this star with whom, I felt, I had a special bond. I was enormously impressed by his rich baritone voice and he was to remain a firm favourite of mine, particularly when Jeanette MacDonald contributed vocal harmony.

Bernard Ratcliffe of Commercial Road continued his commentary of life at the Cinema, and another special pal at that time was Gerald Rowley of the Brook Street area whose family was closely linked to the Rowleys of Dicken Street. Gerald was a classmate at Central School and his great love was for silent films and their history. The life of American film pioneer D W Griffiths had a special appeal for him and he was wonderful to listen to. A year or more later, I remember, he sponsored a visit to the Picturedrome and we saw the Crazy Gang in 'Gasbags'. What a hilarious night we had! Not surprisingly, in adult life Gerald became an award-winning BBC cameraman, and since this honour was achieved throughout the conflict in the Congo (known as Zaire today) he was also a very brave man.

Whenever the Cinema had the same programme for the whole week I missed my Thursday treat since Gran would have been to see the film on the Monday night with my brother Leslie. This irked me, especially if I hadn't the coppers to purchase my own ticket. Three appealing productions I missed in this way were 'Huckleberry Finn' with Mickey Rooney, 'Newsboys' Home' with Jackie Cooper, and 'Stagecoach' with John Wayne. My biggest disappointment of the year was my failure to find the wherewithal to see 'The Adventures of Robin Hood', undoubtedly the peak of Errol Flynn's career. It was first shown early in the year at the Majestic and some weeks later at the Cinema. Its showing at the Cinema was during the first half of the week, so again I had missed out. Years later the film was re-issued and shown at the Regal. Things didn't go smoothly then either. On the night I attended the reels were shown in the wrong order, but this rare novelty was accepted with good humour by the audience. Was there ever a more delectable Maid Marian than Olivia de Havilland? I think not. At least, with the long delay in catching up with the film I had reached an age when I could imagine it was me climbing up the ivy to her window instead of Mr Flynn, and with the same idea in mind!

In late August and throughout September local folk with a bob or two to spare had a bargain chance to see some of their film favourites in the flesh. Robert Donat and the Old Vic Company arrived in Buxton for the Theatre Festival. For a mere five shillings and sixpence Macclesfield patrons had coach transport and a seat in the stalls in the Opera House. Robert Donat had completed filming 'Goodbye, Mr Chips' earlier in the year and would, in due course, receive the Academy Award as best actor for his performance, denying Clark Gable the supreme accolade for his role as Rhett Butler in 'Gone With the Wind'. Robert Donat's supporting cast at Buxton included Constance Cummings, Marie Ney, Stewart Grainger, Sonia Dresdel, Andrew Cruickshank, Max Adrian and Andre Morell.

Two British films shown in Macclesfield during the year were linked, in a remarkable way, to the present day. In April, 'Penny Paradise' featuring Edmund Gwenn was shown at the Picturedrome, and in October, 'Let's be Famous' with Jimmy O'Dea was at the Premier. Each of these films had, as its leading lady, the young, vivacious, Miss Betty Driver who, for close on thirty years has been on our TV screens as Betty Turpin, or more recently Betty Williams, at the Rovers Return, Coronation Street. What a trouper! Turning professional as an eleven-year-old in the thirties, Betty had a singing voice of rare quality. Clear as crystal at all times, sweet, warm and soothing when singing ballads, she had a chirpie and endearing style with more rhythmic numbers. Here's wishing Betty and her devoted sister, Freda, many more years of contentment together.

Following the declaration of war against Germany on September 3rd, 1939, there was never a single moment when I doubted that victory would eventually be ours. Nor did I detect any sign of pessimism in anyone else. It was as if we were bonded in some special way, which indeed we were, for the British spirit, I came quickly to learn, is a potent force to be reckoned with. Naturally, there was unease, for war, even for the victorious, has a dreadful price, but there was a general buoyancy to counteract depression. Life moved up a gear. Film-makers, songwriters, authors, entertainers, volunteers of one organisation and another, everybody who had it in their talent or nature to lessen care in others, did so and our nation was bolstered by it. Local newspapers played their part and hundreds of photographs of service men and women were published through the war years, especially those linking several members of a family to HM Forces. Acknowledgements from grateful service personnel for Mayor's Comforts Fund parcels were a constant news feature also.

Other news was not well received; how loved ones had been lost fighting for our cause but, incredibly, cheerfulness dominated throughout or, at worst, appeared to do so, and that's what mattered.

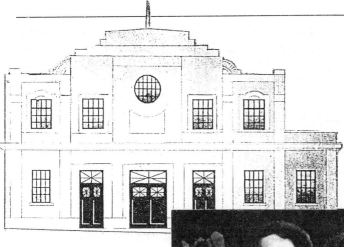

**The facia of the Picturedrome, Chestergate.**

**Mrs Betty Driver, Coronation Street stalwart with a friend. (*Congleton Chronicle*)**

*Below, a 1930s film fare for Macclesfield folk.*

# THE POPULAR CINEMAS OF MACCLESFIELD

| 'Phone 1412 MONDAY, FEB. 20 | MAJESTIC | Free Car Park. All Week | 'Phone 2016 | PICTUREDROME | Free Car Park. |
|---|---|---|---|---|---|
| | | | Monday, Tuesday & Wednesday. | | Thursday, Friday and Saturday. |

A tale of the London Streets! Romance! Humour! Tragedy!

## CHARLES LAUGHTON

IN

# ST. MARTIN'S LANE

with VIVIAN LEIGH, REX HARRISON
Also a Walt Disney Cartoon: "Donald's Better Self"
EARLY BOOKING ADVISABLE.

Matinees: MON. and WED. at 2-30.    Children's Matinee: SAT. at 2-30.

The film version of the play that kept Broadway in tears and cheers for many record breaking months.

DOUGLAS FAIRBANKS Jnr. and GINGER ROGERS in

## Having Wonderful Time

The first of LESLIE CHARTERIS' stories to reach the screen. A thriller of the Edgar Wallace type!

## The SAINT IN NEW YORK

America's Public Enemy No. 1 called to rid New York of the rest of the crooks. There's a thrill every second.

With Louis Hayward & Kay Sutton

Matinee: Wednesday at 2-30.   Saturday (Children's) at 2-30.

| 'Phone 3766. Mon., Tues., Wed., Next. | CINEMA | Free Car Park. Thurs., Fri., Sat., next. | 'Phone 1367. Mon. Tues. Wed. next. | PREMIER | Free Car Park Thurs., Fri., Sat. next. |
|---|---|---|---|---|---|

The inside story of a one-man war on gangland!

### SMASHING THE RACKETS

with CHESTER MORRIS BRUCE CABOT

Also GEORGE O'BRIEN in a Western thriller

### BORDER G-MAN

FIRST TIME IN MACCLESFIELD!

## Bulldog Drummond in Africa

with John Howard, Reg. Denny.
Also
Thrill-packed Hopalong Cassidy drama

## BAR 20 JUSTICE

Hoppy, Windy & Lucky ride again!

Paroled convict—hounded by the law. Is it possible for any such man to "go straight"?

BARTON MacLANE and GLENDA FARRELL in

## PRISON BREAK

Also BOB BAKER in

## Outlaw Express

Invisible danger lurking behind the still form of a murder victim lying in the mortuary. You'll be scared stiff, but you'll love it.

PRESTON FOSTER with

## The CASE OF THE MISSING BLONDE

Also DONALD WOODS in

## Danger on the Air

Evenings: All Week at 6-20.   Mat., Wed. at 2-30. Children's Mat., Sat. at 2-30.

Matinee: Monday and Thursday at 2-30.   Children's Saturday at 2-30.

FILMS FOR TO-DAY AND TO-MORROW:—

MAJESTIC ... ... ... "PYGMALION" with Leslie Howard, Wendy Hiller
CINEMA ... ... ... "KING OF ALCATRAZ" with Lloyd Nolan
PICTUREDROME ... ... ... ... "THE LADY VANISHES"
PREMIER ... ... ... ... "WALKING DOWN BROADWAY"

**The author's melancholy interpretation of the Disney masterpiece that
eluded him. Acknowledgements to Walt Disney Studios.**

## Chapter Twenty-one
### Pinocchio

It was early in 1940 that I was recommended by my pal Philip Harding to take over his duties as delivery boy for Margaret Cockayne who managed her brother Fred's grocers shop at 175 Hurdsfield Road on the corner of Bamford Street. This petite lass, though only a teenager, was as competent as they come, and it is important to remember that food rationing was in vogue with all its associated problems for the retailer. Margaret took it all in her stride with a constantly placid and cheerful temperament and I was, and continue to be, to this very day, greatly attached to her.

She was the youngest of nine children and following the death of her father, who was only 48 at the time, her mother had taken in washing to keep the family's heads above water. I am pleased to report that Mrs Cockayne was still alive and well and assisted in the shop (bought in 1938 and converted from a drapers) when I joined them.

My duties covered Thursdays and Fridays, commencing straight after school and carrying through into early evening. I received five shillings weekly - a generous return, all things considered - which I usually used to purchase whatever small items my mother required for her larder at any given time. An added bonus to the job was the carrier-bike provided. Made from thick tubular steel, heavily lacquered in black, it was built like a tank and was balanced as delicately as a butterfly. It had no gears and the onerous task of pushing this weighty model up hills was more than compensated by the joy of the descent!

Thursdays was confined to visiting established customers with my notebook and pencil and taking their orders for delivery on the morrow. I had two 'rounds'; higher Hurdsfield and Macclesfield Common, in that order. There was little cycling possible between Margaret's shop and the George and Dragon at the summit of Rainow Road and I would cheerfully push the bike up the incline knowing that exhilaration would be my reward in the fullness of time. On an odd occasion I would meet up with Colin Sparks on his red telegraph delivery bike but, far more frequently, it would be Jack Mottershead, similarly employed as Colin, who would alight from his lighter cycle and accompany me on foot.

I had several calls to make in the area at the bottom of Cesterbridge, as I have always known it, although I have yet to see a sign with the name.

I would go up the lane opposite the stonemasons business and call first at the smallholding of Mr and Mrs Hampson whose son Harold was an old Daybrook chum. A most industrious couple were the Hampsons, dad always busy on his land and mum fully occupied in the stone-flagged kitchen. I never once found them relaxing.

Mrs Moon, round the corner in Kerridge Road, lived at 'Rockwood', a bungalow, which had a splendid length of flat front garden. She was a most handsome lady with a beautiful oval face which seemed to advertise benevolence and good health. Her son Jack was married to Hilda Cockayne, Margaret's sister. Mrs Page, Mrs Moon's near neighbour was the last of my calls in that road.

The return journey to the shop from this pleasant area was eminently more pleasurable than the outward trip. The long length of slight incline from the stonemasons could just about be negotiated by pedal power and as I neared the crest of the hill and prepared to take the left turn as the road levelled out I could commence to tick a mental register of boys and girls I knew as I passed their homes on that relaxed return to base. Having passed the George and Dragon on my left I would glance to the houses on the right and perhaps see young, flame-haired Donald Ainsworth before the road began its steep, snaking descent.

With the canal bridge approaching fast as I swept down Rainow Road my thoughts would be of Derek Miles who lived on the left, and then, as I flew over the bridge, of Ronald Sutton on the right, followed within a second or two by the home of Olwen and Ellen Potts and their family, tucked in the short run of cottages between the Britannia Inn and the grocers-cum-post office. Soon, as the road levelled out past the 'Britannia', the Johnson brothers, Gordon, Philip and young Douglas would come to mind on the left immediately following the Higher Fence Road turning. Still on the level and travelling swiftly with Howe Street coming nearer on the right I would be reminded of Norman Stanton, Fred Slater and Sheila Craghill at the corner shop. A gentle descent to Timber Street and a turn or two of the pedals as I climbed slightly again and I could glance right down Pleasant Street where Philip Harding was probably indoors, tweezers in hand, poised over his stamp album, and within yards, with Hurdsfield Church railings on my left as the ground levelled again briefly, I would think of Gordon Cobham and his attractive sisters in one of the cottages on my right. A short descent later with the approach to Margaret's shop on my left, the last mental tick in the register would go to Leslie Nockton at the shop on the upper corner of Bamford Street.

I would be in no rush to tackle the second phase of my duty. While enjoying a leisurely cuppa, I'd watch Margaret dealing efficiently with her regular calling customers, the Bartons, Hackneys, Bentleys, Boultons, Burgesses and Potts; or chatting with her boyfriend, Vernon Corbishley who would often pop in at that time of day. What a wonderful team Margaret and Vernon have proved to be through all the years - may there be many more to come.

My second phase start gave me a freewheel ride down Hurdsfield Road to Arbourhay Street and Fence Avenue which I would ascend on foot, usually with a song on my lips. At the time songs such as Over The Rainbow, We'll Meet Again, There'll Always Be An England, Run, Rabbit Run, The Washing On The Siegfried Line and Bless 'Em All were known by everybody and A Nightingale Sang In Berkley Square would soon be added to the repertoire.

Calls I made in the Macclesfield Common area included Mrs Pointon, just inside Daintry Terrace, Fountain Street, Mrs Baguley, at the top end of Allen Street, Mrs Brierley of the coal merchant family, in Knight Street, Mrs Corbishley (Vernon's mother) in Saville Street and Mrs Holden and young daughter Pauline, in Copper Street. That completed the taking of orders for that week. The next day I would repeat the errand and deliver them their goods and receive payment. I would expect to pay the money into the shop at about 7.30 on Friday evening by which time Margaret had been relieved by her mother. Mrs Cockayne was a trusting lady and would sweep the mass of coins into the counter drawer without checking its accuracy, a practice I was wholly unhappy with. To be at peace in my own mind I would call at my home each week, prior to paying in at the shop to ensure the sum was correct.

Good pals of mine in those early war days included Gerald Poynton, a country-wise lad and his brother Philip, young Stanley Hall, who I loved like a brother, John Wright, Reg and John Challinor, and Sonny Walker. The declaration of war had not made a great deal of difference to Cinemagoers. There had been a brief cessation to theatre and cinema activities but within a week theatres had opened again but with programmes commencing earlier than hitherto, the intention being to clear such places by 10pm or shortly afterwards. Gas masks, as well as tickets, were obligatory in order to gain admittance. Public houses were subjected to a similar curfew. Inevitably, a strictly controlled blackout was imposed and as that year ended and a new one began Granny Talbot and I would trudge the length of Commercial Road and back each Thursday evening, with sickly green luminous discs pinned to our coats. The call of the Cinema, Buxton Road, would not be denied.

As I think back to 1940, highlighted by the epic evacuation of the British Expeditionary Force from Dunkirk in the last days of May and early June and the success of RAF Fighter Command by the end of October in the Battle of Britain, my weekly outings to the Cinema with Gran, whilst enjoyable to a degree at all times, were not enhanced by film quality too often. Notable offerings I can count on one hand. 'Naughty Marietta' in April, 'The Hound of the Baskervilles' and 'David Copperfield' in August and 'The Wizard of Oz' and 'Balalaika' during Christmas week. But if the cinema fare and events of that year engendered no stories worth the telling today, the same cannot be said of my memories - brief as they are - of the Majestic Cinema within that period.

Late one Saturday afternoon during October, Mother disclosed, quite unexpectedly, that she was taking me to the Majestic for the second 'house' that evening. My mother had never been much of a filmgoer and this news was a surprising delight for me. Just as the final night's performance of a stage presentation merits a very special status, so I reasoned attendance at the week's final performance at the town's leading cinema must be considered an event of some magnitude. The tickets were already booked, I learned. What I did not learn, then or afterwards, was the full story - if there was one - of how I came to benefit from such good fortune.

And so, in good time, Mother and I took our seats in the downstairs centre stalls. The film was 'The Grapes of Wrath', based on a John Steinbeck story and was another huge success for film actor Henry Fonda. No doubt my euphoric mood prior to the film's commencement had a great bearing on my enjoyment of it. I was spellbound by the bitter and ironic saga of the farmers and their families' trek from Oklahoma to California in search of a better life during the Depression. What a thrilling evening it was for me! I bubbled animatedly all the way home. I did not know then that reaching a pinnacle of pleasure that night was just the first half of a story, and that within a short time the second part of the tale would unfold. Just a week or two later, I learned from the Macclesfield Times that Walt Disney's 'Pinocchio' was to be screened at the Majestic the following week. There had been plenty of publicity heralding the film's arrival in this country and the beautiful rendering on the radio of When You Wish Upon A Star by light tenor Cliff Edwards, had whetted many an appetite as well as my own. The Pinocchio story was an excellent choice by Disney and I knew the brilliance of the animation was bound to impress me, but it was the superb craftsmanship of the Disney artists which would make seeing the film an experience of magical fantasy. I decided that in order to make the most of the opportunity I would delay seeing the film until the very last performance on the Saturday evening. My wonderful experience of 'The Grapes of Wrath' was an assurance of absolute fulfilment.

It was a pretty long week - but eventually Saturday arrived and I set off in good time, making for the Duke Street entrance to the theatre where the cheaper tickets were sold. I was surprised to find the doors closed and locked, and my knocking brought no response. A passer-by said "You'll have to go round to the front entrance - it's Saturday," so round to Mill Street I went. The Majestic box-office in those days was situated on the left just above the inner steps in the foyer, close to the doors of the auditorium. A small queue had formed, there being some thirty minutes more to wait before the evening's first performance came to an end. During the wait the queue lengthened to the full extent of the foyer and presumably extended down Mill Street. At last, patrons of the first house spilled out and my queue began its forward shuffle. Soon I was at the box-office. I pushed my coppers through the semi-circle of space in the glass and said, "A fourpenny, please."

"You can't have a fourpenny tonight," said the lady. "It's Saturday - full price - eightpence."

This was an unexpected snag. I groped about in my short trousers pockets for the few coppers I still had. They totalled thruppence ha'penny. Thruppence ha'penny! I was just a ha'penny short ....! In a state of shock I recovered my fourpence and withdrew from the window, pondering what to do. Too late to run home to Hurdsfield, I reasoned. I ran my eye down the queue, seeking a known friend. Alas, they were all adults. Well, one thing was for certain: I couldn't bring myself to beg. What I could do, though, was to remain close to the box-office and appear to be as forlorn as I felt! Someone would be bound to ask "What's the matter, son?" and having replied truthfully to the question help would be forthcoming.

The minutes continued to pass and as more and more people shuffled past the box-office and into the cinema proper, droves of pre-booked ticket-holders swept in from the street and I became more and more anonymous and increasingly crestfallen in the confusion - mental and physical - of it all.

Well, the miracle didn't happen. I might have been invisible for what attention was paid to me and when, eventually, the cinema was filled to capacity and 'House Full' announced by the Manager, Mr Lovatt, the queue still stretched out into the street. I couldn't blame anyone but myself. I had paid the price of my ignorance. Still, it wasn't the end of the world, as I said to my Cinema pal, Bernard Ratcliffe, after telling him my tale of woe the following Monday.

"I'll just have to wait awhile and see it at the Cinema when it returns," I said. Bernard shook his head. "You will not see 'Pinocchio' that soon, Geoff," was his reply. "Disney Studios don't operate like that. 'Pinocchio' has gone to be locked away for a long time. Honest. I'm afraid you've missed the boat."

He was right. The first chance I had to see the film (my spell in HM Forces intervening) was many years later by which time I had a young son of my own and I took him to see it at the Majestic. Of course I was tremendously impressed by the film but saddened also with the realisation that had fate been kinder I would have savoured the wonder of it all at the right time - through the eyes, ears and mind of a youngster. Had the story I have told been fiction, a happy ending would have been easy to contrive. But - that's life for you.

## Chapter Twenty-two
## I discover Deanna Durbin

Following Vincent's departure from Central School towards the end of 1939 until I entered into my third and final year there I had managed to avoid anything approaching a collision with Mr Houseman, but it happened one day in the Spring of 1941, and a bizarre story it is.

Central had the occasional use of St Barnabas Hall, Lyme Avenue, a quarter-mile or so from the school up London Road. Following lunch on this day my class had sauntered up to the hall and with several minutes in hand I lagged happily behind the main body of pupils. Having hung my coat in the back corridor of the hall I turned to find Mr Houseman barring my path.

"Do you know the difference between biography and autobiography?" he asked me.

"Yes, sir," I answered confidently, happy to have the opportunity to present a positive front. My affirmative reply was ignored and he began, and I paid full attention to, a discourse lasting two or three minutes.

"Now do you understand?" he asked me, having concluded his piece.

"I beg your pardon, sir, " I felt bound to say, "but you've got it the wrong way round."

"What d'you mean?" he snapped.

"Well, sir, it is an autobiography that is the story of a person's life written by himself. A biography is -"

"Shut up!"

"But, sir -"

"Shut up, shut up, shut up! One more word out of you and I'll make an example of you. Now get to your class."

It transpired the headmaster had charge of my form that afternoon - the only time I ever remember him taking us - and quite enjoyable it was too, but marred somewhat by the anger I felt from his earlier cavalier treatment. Later in the afternoon when we returned to school to be formally dismissed I hung back in the classroom and reported the incident to my form master, Mr Blackford. He accepted my story without question and offered a consoling word.

"Sorry about that, Hunter," he said. "Leave the matter with me. I'll have a word with the headmaster in the morning."

I never heard another word. I concede it is quite astonishing that a headmaster with an MA degree could be confused with a word prefixed by 'auto'. It may be that this incident and many other traits of Mr Houseman's behaviour can be explained. In 1947 he was taken seriously ill and underwent a serious operation to remove a brain tumour. It is possible he had been host to the tumour a very long time, perhaps throughout his years at Central. He never recovered fully from the operation and remained handicapped by physical weakness but continued for many years as Head, calling upon Mr Jackson to wield the cane on his behalf. What Mr Jackson felt about this vicarious role is not recorded.

January, 1941 commenced the year splendidly for Granny Talbot and me with a double treat at the Cinema. 'Blossom Time' with Richard Tauber and 'Escape to Happiness' with Leslie Howard and Ingrid Bergmann. A month later I had a taste of 'live' theatre at the Majestic with the appearance of Norman (Over the Garden Wall) Evans, Donald Peers and supporting artistes. The highlight of the year came in May with the showing at the Majestic of 'Spring Parade' starring Deanna Durbin, the young Universal Studios soprano. I knew little about this gifted young lady at the time but for some months previously I had seen a large photograph of her in Lucking's radio shop window, Sunderland Street, advertising records from her earlier film 'It's a Date'. So, courtesy of the Majestic, I made her acquaintance for the first time.

What a voice! What magic! How totally captivated I was with this winsome miss as she sang Waltzing In The Clouds, It's Foolish But It's Fun, and other songs.

I was coming up to fourteen now and at Barnaby, just days away from my birthday, I took my leave from Central School. I was glad to get away for it had been an unhappy period in my life, paradoxically so, considering the affection I had, and would retain for so many lads. In addition to my own classmates there were a number of boys, senior to me, for whom I reserved a special respect. Bill Lockett, Jim Fairhall, John Knight, Fred Sefton, Douglas Boulton, Tom Baskerville, John Baxter, Arnold Copeland, Bob Lander and Tom Davis come readily to mind.

Early in July Gran and I celebrated my sense of liberation with a trip to the Cinema to see 'Girl of the Golden West', a Jeanette MacDonald and Nelson Eddy musical of sorts. Within days I began my working life with Mr Arthur Cox, baker, of South Street. In fairness, I have to say Mr Cox, father of Bernard, a close school pal, deserved a lad better than myself. I had little

**The author with some of his many records of Deanna Durbin - 'the beautiful and outstanding singer' who captivated him.**

interest in the work in the bakehouse but was happy enough pedalling a carrier bike around all week delivering to shops in the immediate area and to homes over a much wider range. My weekly wage was fourteen shillings which was two shillings more than the union rate. Mother allowed me a half-crown spending money so I was rich!

Following my early start I could usually expect to finish my work each day by 1.30pm which meant I was available for cinema matinees throughout each week. At that time, in addition to children's matinees on Saturdays, the Majestic and Picturedrome opened on Monday and Wednesday afternoons, the Premier on Mondays and Thursdays and the Cinema, Wednesdays only. At this point in my calendar I had a stroke of good fortune. Having decided that I would combine my baker's boy duties with my part-time job at Cockayne's grocers, Margaret allowed me to take possession of the shop's complimentary passes to the Majestic and Picturedrome. It was news to me that such concessions existed but Margaret explained that since the Bamford Street gable-end of the shop was used for displaying the cinemas' posters, free passes were given in return. Margaret added a warning rider to her explanation: when a cinema's poster stated 'Free List suspended', no complimentary entry to see the programme was allowed that week. I was to learn that the suspended clause was applied whenever a really decent film was shown. Understandably, this was an arbitrary ruling to which I was constantly opposed.

Cox's bakehouse was a small, old brick building with a split, stable-style door. My early morning duties were greasing the bread tins and weighing the dough. Bread-baking was a six days per week routine and Tuesdays, Thursdays and Saturdays were hovis, fruit and spice bread days also. Every morning, after the greasing and weighing I would climb into the mixing machine and remove any odd bits of hardened dough with a spatula. I considered the steam loaves as our most attractive product. The mix was the same but lids which slid on and covered the baking tins ensured a smooth golden crust when baked. Shops were supplied early. I had two delivery bikes with greatly contrasting baskets, and a pair of hessian gloves for hygienic handling. The two Misses Lea in Mill Lane who were our best shop customers required the big bike for each morning delivery, whereas the brief trip round Macclesfield Common, starting with Miss Phoebe Broom in Gunco Lane required only the small bike and basket.

One particular morning that July comes to mind. I set off for my short circuit of the common as usual. Up Gunco Lane I called at Miss Broom's sparsely-stocked shop where bible tracts were usually in evidence on the counter; then along Black Road to Mr Tom Cundiff's post office, followed by a free-wheel ride down Windmill Street to Cox's shop in Calamine Street. I was left with a single loaf for Mrs Hartshorn, Snow Hill. As I cycled along Heapy Street with this last call in mind I spotted a biggish lad throwing a paper aeroplane up into the air without any success. At each attempt the plane plummeted, taking the shortest route to earth.

I drew up to the curb and said to the lad, "Not much good, is it?" He agreed. "Have you a spare sheet of newspaper?" I asked him. "I can make one better than that."

He went into his home close to the corner of Snow Hill and moments later reappeared with a whole newspaper. We sat down on the pavement together for several minutes, folding, creasing and shaping pieces of the newspaper. It was, I suppose, a basic form of origami learnt in my Waterloo Street days. The lad, a big and gentle type, was well pleased with the results. His name was Ronald Armstrong and he was three years older than me, and over the next 18 months or so we enjoyed many matinee performances together, usually at the Premier each Monday and the Cinema on Wednesdays. Ron lives at Knutsford now and I see him from time to time. It's good to see him looking so hale and hearty. Naturally, we talk of those happy days gone by.

"GURNETT SMITHY" Nr. MACCLESFIELD.

Gurnett Smithy - an idyllic scene captured for a 1930's postcard

## Chapter Twenty-three
## Bread rounds

Each Tuesday, Thursday and Saturday I pedalled my bread to Sutton-lane-Ends. Whatever the season this delivery was always a pleasure not least because Byron's Lane was an inviting start to the journey and a pleasurable sequel when I returned. Mr Cox's sister, Mrs Nellie Reeves at 44 Byron's Lane was my first customer on that round. The Reeves' had two young sons, Marshal, a lovely boy with curly red hair and Howard who was little more than a toddler. After this call (at the back door, as was often stipulated) as I approached Lindop's shop on the corner of Laburnum Road, I would often see Mrs James busy at her home across the road. She and her husband were Superintendents at the City Mission, Mill Street. From that point on I would enjoy the pleasant length of Byron's Lane before dismounting from my bike at the King's Head, Gurnet, close to where James Brindley master canal builder had served his apprenticeship in the mid-eighteenth century. I had no delivery to make there but I preferred to wheel the bike slowly past the adjoining Smithy. If a horse was being shod or if there was any other activity I would pause for a minute or two and savour the charm of it all. My next deliveries were at the top of Jarman, on the left, firstly at the Geoffrey-Lomases, where the midwife's delivery coincided with my own at one point, and then next door to the Chadwicks with daughter Joan, at 'Jarman Crest', before making the right turn at the Church House to Sutton crossroads and Walker Lane. The short row of cottages on the right after the cenotaph was followed by a patch of garden containing damson trees. Fifty-five years later those trees are still producing fruit.

I would complete my deliveries in Walker Lane ending with a call at the police house. I was calling there when Constable Trynor and his wife moved in and recall the arrival of their first child. A nice gentle freewheel ride down Bullock's Lane would serve to remind me how much better this life was than life at school! As I approached the canal bridge early into my job I spotted several sweet chestnut trees bordering the farm track to the right and pledged to call on them later in the year; then it was down into Byron's Lane again and back to my South Street base.

Moss Rose Estate came next for delivery, starting with Mrs Swindells at the Rutland Road/Moss Lane junction and ending with a call at Detective Sergeant Fearick's home in the Ash Grove area. Some of the calls in between I found disturbing. I had thought we Hunters had been poor in the old days but not like that. Somehow, though, these poor souls scraped the coppers together to pay their way and I had only one customer on the estate who created problems for Mr Cox. This colourful character never disputed she owed money. She just denied so many weeks had gone by since she had last paid! Her insinuations that I had purloined some of her money never troubled me in the slightest. My notebook in which everything was recorded on each doorstep was my advocate and there was nothing more to be said. I was fastidious in the handling of money and enjoyed Mr Cox's full trust.

Back at the bakehouse I would load up again for delivery to homes in the vicinity making several journeys to and from. The Waltons in Byron Street, with their several sons were catered for at this point, as were many residents in High Street, Coronation Street, St George's Street, etc. At what had been the 'Seven Stars' public house in Old Mill Lane I was permitted to enter the front door without knocking and make my way up the long corridor to the living quarters; and across the road, at a house with steps, a cadaverous old woman would settle her weekly bill each Saturday with precise coinage and say, "I'll have to see you again," hinting that a tip would eventually be forthcoming. Her tale never varied, except at Christmas when she would say, "I'll have to see you in the new year". Of course, she never did 'see me' in the way she meant.

My final round of the day was mainly to the north side of town calling first at Hobson Street and Park Lane before making my way to Mrs Wardle at 21 Statham Street and thence to Brown Street and Barton Street to a Mrs Birch, a young mother whose husband was away serving his country. Most names elude me after all these years but my last call in Crossall Street, at about number 69, was to the Hulses with young daughter Margaret. In due course I would arrive in Pownall Street and make my penultimate call at number 90, the home of Mr and Mrs Cunningham and children Winifred, Mary and Gerard. Mrs Cunningham was my favourite customer and I valued her very highly; and with good reason. Unfailingly she would tip me with tuppence every Saturday, and having delivered my last loaf to Northgate Avenue I would make my way to Brock Street, usually about 1pm, park my bike against the kerb of number 34, cross the street to the grocer's shop and buy two sponge cakes in paper concertina cases (probably Palin's or Gaskell's) with Mrs Cunningham's tuppence. I would then return to my bike, sit contentedly on the seat at the kerb and enjoy my treat in celebration of a week's work completed. Once refreshed in this way

I would return, not to the bakehouse which would then be closed, but to Mrs Cox's grocer's shop (a private house at 25 Pitt Street today) to pay in and report to my master.

From an entertainment viewpoint providence continued to work on my behalf. I was given prior notice by Cinema pal, Bernard Ratcliffe of a special occasion in store for me. Commencing on Monday, October 20th, and as part of a nationwide event, the Cinema screened The Deanna Durbin Festival, showing a different film each night for six days enabling me to enjoy a cornucopia of this beautiful and outstanding singer's earlier successes. Shown in a 'growing-up' sequence the films were: 'Three Smart Girls'; 'One Hundred Men and a Girl'; 'Mad About Music'; 'That Certain Age'; 'Three Smart Girls Grow up' and 'First Love' in which Deanna's first screen kiss (lucky Robert Stack!) made world news. I saw every film and that week has to be one of the best of my life. Miss Durbin, with a voice seemingly refined in heaven, is the angel who went to the top of my tree in 1941 and has remained there ever since. If I regretted that week coming to an end it is doubtful if Mr Cox did but he suffered my incessant early morning chatter about the incomparable Miss Durbin with good grace. One major snag working for him was holiday times, particularly Christmas when so much extra work was involved. One's own holiday has to be well-and-truly earned in the baking trade, I learned. My first taste of this pressure came on Christmas Eve 1941, little more than two weeks after the Japanese attack on Pearl Harbour, when the boss and I worked like the clappers throughout the day, he employed doing the baking and I rushing it out to the shops and homes in much greater quantities than normal.. Our day stretched from early morning until 10 o'clock at night. There was some consolation for me. Thanks to my customers' Christmas spirit and I believe, my cheerful and respectful demeanour, I had thirty shillings in tips to show for my cordiality! But it was one hell of a hard slog for the pair of us and I resolved to find myself a job in due course where I could simply 'down tools' prior to holidays, without any additional pressure.

An interesting story is to be told of that Christmas Eve regarding the baking of Hovis bread. Wary of imitations, the Hovis company guarded its product and its good name jealously. 'Merciless' would not be too strong an adjective to describe the action taken against those who sought, spuriously, to benefit from its reputation and in the early years of the Hovis story, courts were kept busy dealing with offenders.

Early that day Mr Cox said, "Take the big bike, Geoffrey, and go to

Mr Coppenhall's. He's expecting you and is giving us a loan of some tins to help us out." Within minutes I was at Mr Coppenhall's bakehouse on Black Road. Since the baking tins fitted inside each other I returned to South Street with a fair load. Both Mr Cox and Mr Coppenhall were renowned for their products. I was never to witness Mr Coppenhall's dexterity but Mr Cox was an absolute genius handling the dough, whether it be one large portion getting the firm symmetrical treatment with the rhythm of both hands or separate smaller portions in each hand. Well, with the pressure of extra baking an error was made and some time later we discovered that a batch of small Hovis loaves had been baked in plain tins and emerged from the oven without identity, whereas the small fruit loaves were proudly displaying 'Hovis' on their sides. I regarded the mix-up with undisguised hilarity at first but Mr Cox was quick to suppress my humour

**Teas with Hovis......a familiar sign up and down the country**

and pointed out that a serious breach of the Hovis code had been made. "Hovis bread," he said, "should have the name written on it, and Hovis tins should have nothing baked in them but a Hovis mix!" We were guilty on two counts! It is to Mr Cox's credit that he was deeply concerned but in the end, we had to take a chance. I was ordered not to bring the matter to the notice of anyone on my delivery rounds and we could only hope that hearty appetites over the next few days would remove all evidence of default. And so it proved.

As a postscript to the events of 1941,the 'live' stage fare available at the Majestic during the second half of that year was:

**August 4th** (one week)       - Blackpool Follies.

**August 25th** (one week)     - Duggie Wakefield and his Gang.

**September 15th** (one week)  - Lilac Time.

**October 13th** (one week)    - Radio Revels, with Stainless Stephen,
                                       Harry Hemsley and Norman Long.

**December 25th** (9 days)    - Bert Loman's Goldilocks and the Three
                                       Bears, in which the song
                                       'Yours' featured strongly.

View over the Royal Silk Warehouse in Waters Green built in 1903. It was home to the Castle Shoe Company for many years and throughout World War II. In 1969, Arthur W Clowes Ltd Printers moved in and remain there to this day. The view looks over the world of the Waterloo Boy with the trees of Victoria Park filling the hindground in front of the countryside.

## Chapter Twenty-four
## The shoe factory

The working pattern of my life in 1941 continued throughout 1942, and being repetitive and uneventful need not be referred to further at this point and I intend to deal only briefly with that year. War news was an important daily diet in our lives. The BBC's Frank Philips and Alvar Liddell (who was also a singer of some note) were names and voices familiar and important to us all. Early in 1942 the Japanese were very much on the offensive, taking Singapore in mid-February and completing their conquest of Burma less than three weeks later. German forces under Rommel gave Hitler something to smile about by taking Tobruk in June but Monty's Eighth Army wiped the smile from the Fuehrer's face later in the year at El Alamein, the swing of the pendulum at this point moving emphatically to the side of the Allies in North Africa.

On the family front, Eileen, the eldest, had already left home to help the war effort as a draughtswoman. Tony, at that time employed as a clerk by Mr Joseph Welch, Coal Merchant of Hibel Road, attained his 18th birthday in July and had hopes of becoming a Fleet Air Arm pilot. On the morale-boosting entertainment front the Majestic went 'live' on three occasions that year. In February 'Variety Parade' was presented with Hatton and Manners; in June 'Radio on Parade' starred Monte Rey with Dickie Henderson and in July 'Radio Fanfare' featured The Two Leslies (Sarony and Holmes), Joe Peterson and comedienne Suzette Tarri. It was also a vintage film year for the Majestic. Their presentations included 'The Great Lie', 'Sergeant York', 'The Chocolate Soldier', 'One of our Aircraft is Missing', 'Babes on Broadway', 'How Green was my Valley', 'They Died with their Boots On', 'Woman of the Year', 'Mrs Miniver', 'The First of the Few' and 'Holiday Inn', in which Bing Crosby saw the old year out and the new year in with Irving Berlin's memorable song, White Christmas.

Early in 1943, as Allied momentum against the Germans moved inexorably to victory in North Africa and this same foe counted winter losses of 500,000 on the eastern front, I was visited at my home by my old Daybrook pal Colin Smith. By now Colin's family had moved from Smyth Street and now occupied what had formerly been The Bird in Hand pub on the corner of Queen Street and Commercial Road, across from the Steam Bakery. Like the bakery door the Smith's front door was set in the building gle across the corner and had narrow swing doors with the bird in ...d motif still displayed in the glass. Colin wanted to know if I fancied a change of job. His fellow 'inker' at The Castle Shoe Company had left, he said, and he had been instructed to seek a replacement. I will not bore the reader at this stage by trying to explain what 'inker' meant but when Colin spoke of "thirty bob a week", I began to take notice as the figure was eleven shillings more than my combined Cox's bakery and Cockayne's delivery wages.

Situated in the fine Robinson Brown building on Water's Green, known as The Royal Silk Warehouse in earlier years, the shoe company was a substantial business linked, I believe, to Proctor's leather business in Pickford Street. I agreed to go for interview and was accepted without fuss. I handed in my notice to Mr Cox and to Margaret at the shop. I had enjoyed a very pleasant year and a half or more since leaving school, much of the pleasure attributed to the complimentary cinema ticket concession from Margaret who was now perfectly happy to accept my move into fuller employment.

Mr Cox was saddened to see me go but although he had been a first-class boss I had never considered it as anything other than a temporary job. Shortly after my departure I was pleased to learn that my Cinema matinee chum Ronald Armstrong was assisting at the bakery with delivery duties.

Castle Shoe's products, when I was with them, were exclusively for the ladies. Every shoe they made had the same platform with the same high heel of chunky thickness, albeit in varying size, the difference being in the variety of upper leather design. More than 90 percent of the shoes were black and the remainder brown. The shoes, each containing a wooden last, were transported about from one process to another on shelved trolleys with small wheels. These trolleys carried several dozen pairs of shoes at a time and each trolley was docketed with full information of its load to enable the work's office and the piece-workers to record output. I was most impressed with the finishing room's piped vacuum system which incorporated every cutting and sanding machine in the department. Operated by a giant fan at the rear of the company's premises, it ensured that all waste pieces and particles of dust incurred in trimming and sanding operations were sucked away instantly.

I was placed alongside Colin at his bench in the finishing department situated on the first floor of the building and when each trolley reached us the soles and heels had been trimmed and smoothed and were ready to be stained to the colour of their uppers - which is where Colin and I came in. Using either black or brown dye our task was to swiftly apply the dye to the sole and heel edges, getting well into the 'nicks', without contaminating the upper leather. For this purpose we held two brushes simultaneously in the hand. The first was like a biggish wooden tooth-brush held in the normal way between index finger and thumb. The second was a small, flat brush held at right angles to its partner between the third and little finger. The handles of both brushes crossed and were gripped in the palm of the hand. This method was favoured to ensure a high speed of operation.

A shoe would be gripped by its upper at the heel in the left hand, the tooth-brush dipped in the tin of stain and applied to the sole edge. The shoe was then tossed gently into the air and caught upside-down. Both brushes were then primed with stain, the tooth-brush applied high on the heel close to the upper and the broad brush completed the painting of the heel.

It was a messy, smelly job requiring overalls and apron but Colin and I were a contented team and spent much of each day singing songs together. Our department's foreman was Mr Austin Abbott, a competent, friendly chap with no superior airs, and I grew very fond of him. The big boss was Mr Ted Millett, who wore a white 'slop' coat and an authorative air at all times. An astute organiser, he was the father of Fred Millett, a lad my own age, who was 'cricket mad' even in those days and was to earn a considerable reputation in the sport.

I was pleased to find that Mr Adam Hope, the Scout-master from my Barracks Square days was employed there as store-keeper and supplied our brushes and dyes. Others I remember are Arthur Bowers, Herbert Galley from Bank Street, Fred Crohn, young Leslie's father from St George's Street, Dennis Millett (Ted's brother), Dennis Malkin, George Gallimore, Neville Skinner, Colin Howarth, Dennis Barker, Jack Shepherd and Clarence Massey, who married one of the Newton girls from No 8 Crew Avenue.

Most other men in the finishing department were mature piece-workers and we two inkers were sandwiched between operatives eager to relinquish trolleys to us on the one hand, and hungry to accept them on the other, so there could be no dawdling, and it was very much a 'treadmill' existence for all concerned.

April of that year is well remembered by me. During the week linking March to April the Majestic screened Road to Morocco, the third film in the Crosby/Hope/Lamour series, and the song 'Moonlight Becomes You' became a repetitive rendering for Colin and me, to the consternation of our workmates. Also, during that month, I joined the Army Cadet Force at the King's School. This was to prove one of the best decisions I have ever made. Parading at 9am each Sunday morning was no problem but to finish work on a Wednesday evening at 6pm and to wash, have my tea and line up with the other lads at 7pm was something of a rush but I was determined to do it. That first Wednesday evening proved to be opportune. Captain Walker, a short, plump chap invited volunteers for a Saturday afternoon cross-country race through the Bollin Valley and I couldn't resist the challenge. On the day, John Poolford led the race throughout with me hanging on to second place. I forget now who came third (but I bet he remembers John Poolford and me!) and at the informal presentation of awards ceremony the three of us were each given a lucky stone. Mr Walker then asked John if he would care to sell his stone for ten shillings, which John did. I was asked if I would exchange mine for seven shillings and sixpence, which I was happy so to do. The third lad accepted five bob for his. This strange performance, it seems, was to protect our amateur status.

This early display of generosity endeared me to Captain Walker but, in a very short time, I was to feel genuine affection for all the officers and senior King's School boys who controlled our training. Make no mistake about it, we lads were being prepared for war, quite seriously, but our training was enjoyably challenging. Our presence at each mustering was entirely voluntary but the variation in our military syllabus and the quality of the instruction we received from our regular staff and, for example, guesting Home Guard personnel, meant most cadets stayed the course, and therein lay the success of a project so valuable to our country.

Our Commanding Officer was Major Ransley, a King's master, and in addition to Mr Walker he was ably supported by fellow master Mr Harvey. There was also a young Mr David Watson who, it was claimed, was a member of the much-respected optician family. Quality King's School boy NCOs included Michael Crowder, who remains to this day the finest Regimental Sergeant Major I have ever known, Brian Pickford of Brock Street, whose father was linked to the Alma Cork Company, Crompton Road, Alan Whittington, whose charming sister Audrey enhanced many a social evening, and Peter Robinson of the Lowerfield Road area. This latter cadet must not be confused with the Drum Major of our bugle band, Peter Forbes Robinson, who was usually in evidence on Sunday mornings. He was destined for much greater things than throwing a mace in the air, as his outstanding bass voice was to prove, and carrying the big drum and beating a regular tattoo was my old school chum, Eric Mellor.

Sharing King's School space with the Army Cadet Force was the Air Training Corps. They also had a bugle band and a drum major of rare quality in Sidney Blackshaw, a particularly handsome, blond young man.

What good times they were! Quite decently clothed in our khaki, always we marched up and down for a spell before receiving classroom instruction in weaponry, map reading and infantry field tactics. Town lads I shared these pleasures with, then or later, included Graham Naden, Ken Clayton, Brian Cockayne, Ken Watson, Ernie Slack, Reg Biggar, Roy Booth, Jim Mottershead and Ted Cook. The last two named combined with me at a later date to form a signals instruction team under Captain Ewan Cameron, an ex Royal Corps of Signals officer, in business locally as a shirt manufacturer at Lower Heys, Macclesfield. When the Company had been dismissed on a Wednesday evening a few of us would make a bee-line for the canteen on the first floor of Burton's, Mill Street. Run by the WVS for HM Forces, a few pence would buy beans on toast or pikelets with jam. A coin in the bar billiards machine ('Russian Bagatelle', we called it) provided good sport. When Sunday morning parade ended at 12 noon we would adjourn to Granelli's Chestergate, for thick milk shake and wafer biscuits. The Sunday evenings of those days had much going for them. The 'Monkey Run', as it was called, was a regular feature with lads and lasses parading Mill Street and Chestergate with regular stops for coffee at the Spa Milk Bar, Mill Street - my group favoured the slightly elevated small back room - the YMCA in Derby Street and, of course, Granelli's.

This advertisement from the early years of the century shows what an illustrious past
this fine building has had.

## Chapter Twenty-five
## A career change

As 1943 progressed war news continued to be good. In mid-May the Barnes Wallis bouncing bomb was used to destroy the Rühr Dams and early in the second half of the year, as Allied forces invaded Sicily, my inker partner at Castle Shoe, Colin, informed me of his intention to leave the company once he had served his notice. His decision should not have been the shock to me that it was. After all, inking was an unpleasant operation and it was to our credit that we had maintained a cheerfulness in tandem. I wished Colin well for the future.

Looking back to those days when I was engaged in so mundane a task and accepting an apparent aimless route in life, it is hard to believe that ahead of me was a long fulfilling life as a respected textile artist (if I might modestly make the claim), with a penchant, in later years, to digress as a free-lance cartoonist with a regular newspaper slot.

Now that I was alone at the inking bench I presumed the increased speed of the treadmill life would be transitory and that a new partner would be found for me but after two or three weeks as a single operative I complained to my foreman, Mr Abbott.

"You seem to be coping very well on your own, Geoff," he pointed out. "I am coping with difficulty," I countered. "If I am not to be found a partner to share the load then I want an increase in my wage." Mr Abbott promised to have a word with Mr Millett and he came to see me.

"What's the problem?", he asked.

The problem, I said, was that I and a colleague had been receiving thirty shillings each per week. My colleague had now gone, I was doing it all, and was getting the same thirty shillings for the double duty.

"Don't forget, Hunter," he said, "you are still only working the 49 hours each week that you worked before and you are still being paid the same for the same number of hours."

"That is true, Mr Millet," I conceded, "but before, when I wanted a pee I could go for it. Not now, with all this work to cope with. I am working through my tea breaks to keep the trolleys rolling and have to hang on till dinner-time or tea-time before I can gain any relief."

"I take your point," said Mr Millett. "I'll give the matter some thought and come back to you."

A few days later he returned. "How d'you fancy going on to piece rate?" he asked me.

"That depends ....." I answered cautiously.

"Well, look. Let's give it a try," he said. "I've studied the figures and I can offer you a penny per dozen pairs, for black shoes, and three ha'pence, per dozen pairs, for brown. You can start this coming Monday. Here's a notebook for you to keep your own record of work done."

When he had gone I did my own sums. Talk of 'per dozen pairs' didn't fool me for one moment. A dozen pairs was twenty-four shoes and to earn each shilling I would have to paint 288 black soles and 288 heels. Also I was in no position to influence output and my wage would be governed by the amount of work that came my way in any given week.

It was probably purely coincidental but that first week chanced to be the busiest I had known in the few months I had been at the factory. It was sheer hell keeping up with the pace of production, but by the following Saturday noon my notebook indicated I would receive a wage of fifty shillings in the next Friday's packet - a full pound more than normal. But that week proved to be a flash in the pan and for several weeks after my remuneration averaged about thirty-five shillings; not a return I could accept on a long term basis, given the pressure I was under.

I complained again to Mr Abbott and as a result Mr Millett came to see me again. He had to come to me each time for I did not dare leave my post and allow trolleys to crowd up at my bench. It was a Wednesday and I was eager to seek a compromise before a new week commenced. I told him of my dissatisfaction. I made the point that three ha'pence per dozen for brown shoes was nonsensical as hardly any browns were being produced, three ha'pence per dozen pairs for both black and brown would suit me fine. He pursed his lips and made a whistling sound and shook his head from side to side. "Can't do that," he said. "You're asking for a 50 percent increase."

"Well, how about us forgetting piece-rate. Pay me a flat rate of two pounds a week, Mr Millett, and I'll be happy." He shook his head again with an air of finality. "I think I've been fair enough with you, Hunter. Let's leave things just as they are." And off he went.

On the evening of the next day, casting an inquisitive eye over the situations vacant columns of the Macclesfield Times I spotted that Lonsdale and Adshead Brewery, Park Green, needed a strong boy to assist in their wines and spirits department so at lunchtime next day I stripped off my overalls, made my way to Park Green and climbed the steps to the brewery offices. I was lucky to find the Managing Director, Mr G F Barlow available and offered him my services.

I answered several questions and then he asked, "Are you Tommy Hunter's lad?" and having assured him this was so he said, "Well, you should be able to keep your fingers to yourself. The wage is thirty-five shillings a week and the job's a damn sight cleaner than the one you're doing. Can you start Monday?" "Yes," I answered decisively.

At 11.55 on Saturday morning I broke the news to Austin Abbott that he would not be seeing me there again. Decent man that he was, he remonstrated with me. I was leaving without giving notice - it wasn't the done thing. I apologised but told him I felt very strongly that I was being exploited and had done all I could to reach an agreement on terms. Now that opportunity had beckoned I intended to think of myself and accept it.

My story of the Castle Shoe company does not quite end there. On the following Friday my mother called at the factory to collect my last wage and employment cards and she reported the story to me that evening.

"I spoke to Mr Millett," she said. "He said how very sorry he was to lose you. He said you have been the very best lad he's ever had. And the last thing he said to me was this: 'Mrs Hunter, if it was a question of Geoffrey wanting more money, why didn't he open his mouth?'"

I had to laugh at that.

A post-war picture of Park Green Brewery in the process of demolition. The main brewing premises are on the left and the wines and spirits department is the tall-windowed section to the right of it.

## Chapter Twenty-six
## The Brewery

My first day as an employee of Lonsdale & Adshead's was as easy a baptism to a new job as it was possible to have. Having climbed the steps to their main office on Park Green I was greeted warmly by the wines and spirits manager, Mr A E Lea and taken down a flight of wooden steps to his department at ground level. The store's small office contained a high desk and stool belonging to Mr Lea and a smaller desk and ordinary chair for my use. Mr Lea's tall desk and stool was typical of those in the firm's main office; very Dickensian in appearance with all clerks perched up high and facing blank walls. Pen-holders, nibs and ink-wells were standard equipment. The desk I was to occupy for periods of my duty was the exception to the rule. I faced the window looking out on to Park Green. The bottom half of the window was sand-blasted but when I stood up I could survey the passing scene. Facing me square-on were the public toilets (entrances were at the sides in those days) but trees and their foliage on each side, especially in sunlight, presented an attractive picture.

We had one main square room with an incredibly high ceiling and the need for such height would become evident to me in due course. At the back of this room a stillage of stout timbers had been built upon which stood three of the largest wooden casks I have ever seen. Half as tall again as a man, generously girthed, and with a brass tap at each base, they were highly varnished, had black enamelled hoops and were a most impressive sight. Only the centre one was in use containing the brewery's own brand of whisky. Those three casks must have been assembled in that room by the cooper for there was no other way they could have got there. This centre cask's whisky was not only bottled in the normal way but supplied in bulk to leading hotels in large earthenware jars encased in wicker-work.

Elsewhere in the room, wherever there was wall space, there were shelves stacked with bottles of whisky, brandy, rum, gin, cocktails, and wines, fortified and otherwise. The floor space was also filled substantially with cases of drink and various sized casks. The cellar beneath also contained casks of wines and spirits earmarked for the Lonsdale & Adshead label.

Mr Lea, known familiarly as Ernest to his friends was a family man about 40 years old at this time. He was an easy man to get along with and explained what my duties would be. Firstly, I would have control of the Customs & Excise business of the department. This sounded both grandiose and frightening to me at first but proved to be a fairly simple procedure. By law, all incoming spirits had to have an accompanying Customs & Excise certificate. Details had to be entered in a ledger and the certificate filed. Conversely, all spirits leaving the department for delivery to the brewery's public houses had to have a certificate covering the full amount. Books of these certificates were supplied by the local Customs & Excise office on Hibel Road. Such certificates were usually folded thinly and tied round the neck of a bottle for convenience.

I was also to make up all the orders for the public houses, ready for the waggoners, as we called the draymen, after they had first loaded their vehicles with the hogshead's of beer and crates of bottled ales and stout. My duties would also encompass those of bottler, when required. The brewery had its own brand of whisky, rum, port and red wine, and included in bottling duties would be corking, capsule-sealing - they had an ingenious hand-operated gadget for this - and labelling.

When railway-man Fred Broadhead delivered consignments to us on his horse-drawn cart I was to don an apron and assist him getting the goods inside. John Haig, whisky distillers of Markinch, Scotland, for example, dispatched 40 cases each month to us, so Fred was grateful for my assistance. When signing for goods, at all times I had to write 'Contents unexamined', to enable a claim to be made should any of the order be missing or broken. I was also expected to utilize shelf space constantly and I recall that I stood so many bottles of White Horse whisky on 'parade' that, in no time at all, I could recite, word for word, the complete text of the stagecoach advertisement on the label which began, 'All that are desirious to pass from EDINBURGH to LONDON or any other place on their road .....', and ended with the date, February, 1754!

The general cleanliness of the department was my province as well. I was to sweep the store daily and mop once weekly. My description of the stock would seem to indicate that the topers of those times were well provided for. This was far from being the case and supplies were well below peace-time requirements. Supplies to public houses were rigidly controlled. Had a member of the public been able to purchase a proprietary bottle of Scotch whisky from a legitimate retail outlet the price would have been 25 shillings and 9 pence, equal to close on £40 today, which makes today's tipple a bargain.

Beneficial to me was a 5.30pm finish each day. I was becoming more and more keen and involved in my Army cadet role and could prepare for evening duties at a more leisurely pace. All in all, then, I was entitled to feel I had taken a step or two up the ladder with this new job. This would also be true in a literal sense, as I shall explain when I return to this subject.

As near as I can judge after the passing of so many years it was about the time I took up my new employment at the brewery that my brother Tony returned home in frustrated mood. He had experienced life in the Fleet Air Arm at Lee-on-Solent, for which branch of the Services he had volunteered as a prospective pilot the previous year. He had performed well throughout the course - or had, up to the point of his solo flight. He was certainly a high flyer as a mathematician, but if Tony's performance in the air on that fateful day had lacked the grace necessary to impress his peers, his ungainly landing evidently confirmed their doubts about his prowess. He was asked politely to go - and to close the hangar door behind him!

Undaunted, he had applied to the Royal Air Force for pilot-training and spent some time at Scarborough on an assessment course. That body of our armed forces' enthusiasm for his services extended to offering him a position on the ground staff, which Tony declined and he returned home to plan his next move. A regular pal of his at that time was Jack Bowyer. Jack, who lived on Nicholson Avenue had joined the RAF and became a Flight Sergeant. He would often visit our home when he had a weekend pass and needed no persuading each time to 'tickle the ivories' for us. He was a brilliant pianist and could play the Warsaw Concerto just like Louis Kentner who recorded the piece for the film 'Dangerous Moonlight', a World War 2 story starring Anton Walbrook and Sally Gray. 'In a Persian Market' and Hoagy Carmichael's 'Stardust' were other gems in Jack's extensive repertoire.

I was now achieving double personal satisfaction with my job at Lonsdale & Adshead and my full commitment to the Army Cadets at King's School. There was one period about that time when I was chosen for a physical training course in the King's gym, in Coare Street. This course, conducted by a regular army sergeant named Smith of the Army Physical Training Corps, held on Monday to Friday evenings seemed to last for several weeks and I loved every minute. We had frequent all-day Sunday 'schemes', as they were called, searching for the enemy in the countryside between Macclesfield and Wilmslow, and returning in the late afternoon contentedly exhausted. Social evenings were arranged now and then and the lasses of the Girls' Training Corps would be invited to join in the fun. My name bank offers a poor return here. I can recall only little Dorothy Tinsley and Margaret Davenport, who worked in Jackson's baker's shop, Mill Street and later married Roy McCarthy, well known today for his travel coach business. There was also a girl named Joan, a friendly type who deserves more than my obscure reference. A pleasing feature of the cadet social evenings was that our commanding officer, Major Ransley, always made a point of bringing Mrs Ransley and young sons Christopher and David to circulate among the cadets and make, and partake, of the cocoa! The Ransley family's presence had such a warming influence on the company and was so appreciated by me personally that I have been privileged to enjoy a deep friendship with Christopher and David beyond the lives of their caring parents.

There was one social evening at King's School I remember more than any other. It was held either on a Friday or Saturday evening and to this very day I ponder whether the whole evening was planned as one event or whether two separate functions coincided to the cadets' - boys and girls - benefit. During the evening I chanced to wander into the school's main hall and was surprised to find a musical concert taking place and I quietly took a seat to enjoy this unexpected bonus. There were more surprises in store for me. Major Ransley took the stage and gave a fine tenor rendering of Handel's 'Where E'er You Walk'. Following this treat an established favourite of mine, young and beautiful soprano Gladys Parry, who lived on Brunswick Hill, and was employed by Brocklehurst Whiston sang 'Trees' and 'Because'. As I write of Major Ransley and Gladys now they are remembered with much warmth and that evening they shared the King's School stage is a treasured memory. About this time also, aware of my lack of social grace, I invested a modest weekly sum in dancing lessons at Bessie Sutton's little studio over a shop in Brunswick Street. My teacher, for the most part, was Mary Twigg, who knew her stuff, and this new accomplishment added further confidence to my demeanour and I considered it money well spent. One girl dancing partner of those war years stands out more than any other even though I knew her only casually. Jessica Ledgar was employed behind the counter of the post office in Sunderland Street. To dance with Jessica was to float on cloud nine!

As 1943 neared its end I continued to count my blessings in my role as assistant wines and spirits storekeeper at Lonsdale & Adshead. I had little contact with the main office where Miss Tilly Boston, a near neighbour of mine in Crew Avenue, was secretary. The officer manager - and very firm in his control - was Mr Fred Walker of Crompton Road, and included in his staff was Mr Jack Hopwood, the former Hurdsfield Road grocer, and two office lads slightly younger than me, Eric Jackson and Norman McGuinness, close friends of mine to this day, with whom I shared firewatching duties. My boss, Mr Lea, was now trusting me with checking his ledger figures, and what a joy the pages of those ledgers were to my sight; such exquisite penmanship I had never seen before. On odd occasions, mid-morning, I would be sent across Park Green to Russell's butcher shop for two hot meat and potato pasties. On other mornings, Jim Reade, the boiler man, who lived in Lowe Street, would send me on the same errand with the same incentive so I was not lacking in sustenance!

One morning Mr Lea came into the store-room and said, "Geoffrey, you're going to learn something new today." He slapped a large cask with his hand and continued, "Now that Christmas is approaching it's time the contents of this big fellow were transferred to the big cask. Go up the yard and pass on my compliments to Tat Hyde and ask him if he can spare us a bit of his time early this afternoon. He'll know what you mean." Up the yard I went to the cooper's shop of Mr Hyde, a master of his craft. In the few months I had been at the brewery I had come to look upon barrels as wonderful creations and I envied young Geoffrey Moss of the Fountain Street area his apprenticeship with Mr Hyde.

Why Mr Hyde was called 'Tat' I do not know. I delivered the message to him and following lunch his aproned figure appeared through the store's rear door. First the cask of proof whisky burn-branded with 'Leith' on its end was tapped, having first been bored with a brace and bit, and given a small vent hole, and then, with a block and tackle it was raised to head height and had a rubber tube attached to the tap and thence threaded into the top of the giant cask against which a firm wooden ladder had been placed. The Leith cask, the size of a hogshead, was then raised further to enable gravity to play its part. With this operation completed the cask was lowered to the floor, the tube disconnected, the grips and chains uncoupled and the tap removed. Carefully the cask was upended over a large brass jug to drain out the last of the proof spirit. I was surprised to note the whisky was a faint straw colour. I suggested to Mr Lea that a pint of water swished around the cask would guarantee the firm getting its full money's worth. When Mr Lea spoke I was reminded of my former boss, baker Arthur Cox and the lecture I had been given regarding Hovis tins.

"It's against the law to add water to one of these casks," he said. "When a whisky cask is first used the wood absorbs a good deal of the whisky content. Now that we have drained the cask, Mr Hyde will seal the tap hole with a firm bung and peg the vent and it will be returned to Leith for another filling without being cleansed in any way. And that's how the cask will be treated throughout its life.

"Now, Geoffrey," continued Mr Lea, "it's your turn. I have calculated how many gallons of water need to be added to the big cask. Put the big wooden tun-dish in the top of the cask, keep filling the one-gallon jug, mark each gallon off at the bottom of the steps - there's a pencil and a paper with the markings - climb up the steps and pour the water in. Keep doing that until the full quota of water has been added and then report back to me."

For the next stage of the operation Mr Lea produced a long wooden pole two inches thick and about 15 feet in length and with this I stood on top of the cask and stirred ... and stirred ... and stirred. After a while, a measure of caramel colouring was added, having first been thinned in a small quantity of the whisky. Then the stirring began again - for ages, it seemed to me - until Mr Lea was satisfied. A final check with his hydrometer confirmed the whisky's specific gravity was correct. The cask's cover was replaced and a period of settling time was all that was required to allow the whisky to clear.

Army cadets NCOs, Jim Mottershead and Ted Cook are shown in this 1944 photo with Capt. Ewan Cameron. The author, then a sergeant, completed the quartet.

King's School.

Kings School, Macclesfield

## Chapter Twenty-seven
## Army cadet

The first few weeks of 1944 brought good news on all war fronts. Allied troops fought their way ashore at Anzio and made headway in the Pacific. The RAF bombed Berlin and Russian troops re-took Kharkov, Smolensk and Kiev and continued their advance westwards. On the Army Cadet front at King's School there was talk of examinations. 'War Certificate A' was a new term to me and I paid little attention to the King's pupil cadets as they discussed their chances of success. Later, though, it became known that the War Certificate examination was in two parts and that most of us lads would be taking Part 1 on a Sunday - soon, and the more experienced would take Part 2 as well a week later. The tests would cover all aspects of our training and the examiners would be regular Army officers. On the Wednesday before the Part 1 examination, Capt Walker spoke to my platoon. There were two remaining places available to contest the Part 2 examination on the Sunday week. He selected six 'most promising' cadets for a special test that evening and I was lucky to be included. He led us to a classroom in the old school and began firing map-reading questions at us. Thanks to Mr Jackson, my old geography master at Central, I had a good grounding in the subject and had taken the trouble to learn all the definitions by heart. Mental arithmetic questions relating to compass errors and magnetic variation held no fears for me either and I was one of the two selected for the event. Before returning home that evening Capt Walker plied us with a good selection of War Office pamphlets, all marked 'secret', for concentrated home study.

I remember nothing of the first exam. The second part a week later I recall being something of a nightmare! I had studied my pamphlets long and hard but had virtually no practical experience at all. I did my stint, marching a squad up and down, barking orders in the approved way - I'd been on the receiving end of that enough to learn something from it - but it was in my role as section leader in the Bollin Valley that I had to disguise my lack of confidence the most. The enemy, I was informed, was approaching Macclesfield and the destiny of our ancient borough was in my hands! All I could do was apply commonsense and hope for the best. I briefed the 'men' in my section with the information I had been given and placed them and my LMG (Bren light machine gun) along the ridge we were to defend and with my fingers crossed explained to the examiner my reason for each positioning. I deliberately chose to be unorthodox in the placing of my LMG to convey original thinking to the examiner but he remained poker-faced throughout. The day, the tests and the ordeal stretched to late afternoon and finally I was alone with the map-reading examiner. I did my parrot chant when definitions were asked for, took a compass reading of the school gates in fading light, threading my thumb through the compass ring in the prescribed manner, converted the reading to a back-bearing and completed by locating my position on a map with ruler and protractor.

My own assessment of the day was that I had done quite well with the map-reading and had made a complete botch of everything else, and in my prayers that night I thanked God for getting me through the agony of the day. I asked no favours and have often thought since, in view of what happened, He must have approved of my attitude. The memory of that day was revived some weeks later when I turned up for Wednesday night parade to be told I had passed both parts of the examination and been awarded the certificate. My unexpected success caused quite a stir for it qualified me for immediate promotion to full corporal. Capt Walker who had shown me so much kindness throughout the year, had suffered the disappointment of failing Part 2 of the examination. Although the impartiality of the examiners was commendable, I was saddened that he had been hurt in this way for he had not needed to participate at all. My sudden rise from obscurity to prominence did not go unchallenged. In an interview with Mr Harvey, a lieutenant, I met his comment "You'll have to smarten yourself up, Hunter, if you're going to wear two stripes on each arm" with a gentle tug of the horse-collar tunic I was wearing and the retort, "A uniform that fits would go a long way to achieving that, sir!" He smiled and nodded. "I must have a word with the Quartermaster about you," He was as good as his word.

No sooner did I have the two stripes on my sleeve than the town company, placed under the command of Capt Francis Bullock, a leading hairdresser in Cross Street, transferred from King's School to Springfield, Byron's Lane. Major Ransley continued as supremo. Mr Bullock was another good company commander. Firm and flexible, with a good sense of humour, he and I got on famously. He had no doubts about my ability and within a year he would make me his company sergeant-major. With my contented job at the brewery and such responsibility on the social front also, I was now well set on a more direct and satisfying path in my life.

On June 6th, 1944, D-Day, the Allied invasion of Normandy began and reprisal German V-1 bombs soon began to fall on Britain. By early July, one million US and British troops had crossed the English Channel, the most stupendous enterprise in the history of warfare. The city of Minsk fell to the Russians and US bombers had Tokyo within their range.

On a lighter note, my life at the brewery continued blissfully and in the course of my duties there I made many new friends. One such was Herbert Widdows, a quaint character employed cleaning the beer barrels in the covered area of the yard which was always awash with flowing water and where clogged footwear was essential. Herbert was a very little chap, wizened, and as close as you could get to a leprechaun in appearance. His claim to past fame, was that he had been a champion backwards runner in his younger days. The reader may well ponder why anyone would wish to run backwards. The answer to that, perhaps, is that Herbert, standing about four feet four inches in his clogs when I knew him, could hardly have competed with any success as a frontwards runner. He insisted he had been uniquely gifted as a reverse sprinter and had enjoyed much success; I accepted this wonderful little man's story without question.

I compiled the wines and spirits orders for the brewery's houses. For this purpose I used wooden beer crates which were in plentiful supply and chalked on the crate-ends the names of the landlords and licensed premises. Once completed, the orders were placed in a small whitewashed room with a large green door which for security reasons only opened from within onto the firm's long forecourt on Park Green. The brewery's waggons, having been loaded with their hogsheads and crated beers inside the yard would call at the front on Park Green for the wines and spirits orders. Usually there were two waggoners per vehicle, driver and mate, and occasionally an extra man when deemed necessary. I liked these waggoners. There was never any of the off-hand treatment a lad can suffer from adults; I was treated as an equal. There was gentle giant Jack Bolshaw, a most commanding figure, Len Pickering from Chadwick Terrace, Fred Morton from Nicholson Avenue, Dennis Reade, Tom Holland, Albert Birtles, Jack Morris and Bill Goodier, who had a knack of regularly winning on Littlewood's three draws pool. Memories of my chalking of the crates have remained with me and the following list is a reminder of the days when pint pots reigned supreme.

| | | | |
|---|---|---|---|
| J J Bailey, | Traveller's Rest | J Flanagan, | Sceptre Hotel |
| Herbert Barnes, | Berrisford's Vaults | Sally Hodkinson, | Derby Arms |
| Mr Bowers, | Oxford Road Hotel | Mr Illingworth, | Swan With Two Necks |
| Archie Bradbury, | Blue Bell | Alexander King, | Feathers Inn |
| G Byron, | Post Office Hotel | R A Kinsey, | Black's Head |
| L Copestick, | Green Dragon | Chas Lomas, | Castle Inn |
| Jim Edge, | Waterloo Inn | Reuben Machin, | Mechanics Arms |
| Isaac Green, | Pack Horse Hotel | L Mason, | Bear's Head |
| | (Market Place) | Mr Newton, | Wharf Inn |

The Swan with Two Necks, Chestergate, in the 40s; one of the many local Lonsdale and Adshead 'houses' in the centre of Macclesfield.

## Chapter Twenty-eight
## A happy ending

It was in July, 1944, about the time Hitler survived an attempt to assassinate him, that Vincent, who had been called up for army service in May, was selected to join the Royal Armoured Corps at Barnard Castle, County Durham. Soon afterwards, Tony, who had been in a state of limbo for some months following his rejection by the RAF, volunteered successfully to join Vincent. This pleased the family for it meant the two could come home together at weekends when passes were available. Tony's girl-friend, Joyce Yomans of Bank Street, an attractive, auburn-haired lass who Tony was to marry a year later, dutifully visited our home each Sunday evening while Tony was away. To me fell the chivalrous task of escorting Joyce home in the blackout, taking the short route via the full length of Fence Avenue.

The walk, pleasant in daylight with Victoria Park and its trees, verdant lawns and flower beds, took on a forbidding aspect to a young seventeen year old when shrouded in darkness, especially since the railings had been sacrificed for the war effort. I, for one, regretted the decision to remove the park railings which stretched for hundreds of yards along Daybrook Street and Fence Avenue and included the gates to upper and lower parks and what we termed the 'puzzle gates' on Fence Avenue. I recall the shock I felt when I first saw the railings had gone. All that remained were half-inch jagged stumps sticking out of the smooth rounded concrete sets. These sharp remnants, which were made safe later, had an assortment of electric colours, evidence of the oxy-acetylene flame's work.

I know there were strong arguments for and against this act and the subject had been well aired in the town's council chamber, but I was personally opposed to the loss. To me, those railings were a symbol of the dignity and discipline of the times. They were not a mere peripheral appendage to the park but part of its grand design and should have been allowed to remain standing proudly as an act of defiance against Adolph Hitler and his hateful regime. The other point of view, of course, had to be respected but I have been more aware, through the years, of what we have lost rather than what contribution was made to the War effort.

As the war in Europe continued to rage in the second half of the year, the Germans fought a hard rearguard action. Paris was retaken on August 25th by the Allies and Brussels in early September, but British paratroopers dropped at Eindhoven and Arnhem suffered heavy losses and the German offensive in the Ardennes (the Battle of the Bulge) caused serious losses to the US army.

My cinema visits had declined due to my army cadet duties. Added to normal company parades were my attendances with pals Ted Cook and Jim Mottershead at Capt Ewan Cameron's signals instruction evening and teaching morse code and signals to cadet units beyond Macclesfield. Visits to the Cinema with Granny Talbot had come to an end also. Now in her mid-70s, Gran preferred to stay in her chair by the fire and at 9.30 each evening she would enjoy a pint of mild beer in a quart jug supplied by the Durham Ox. She would pour the beer, one inch at a time, into a small white tea-cup and sip it daintily. She was to continue this pleasant ritual up to the age of 93 when she passed away peacefully in her bedroom.

With the approach of Christmas, a stage show to bring back memories was presented by Brocklehurst Whiston's Weaving Department in aid of the Comfort's Fund. 'Ruti Revue' held in the Pavilion, Fence Avenue, commenced on Wednesday evening, December 13th for four nights. Members of the company were:- Dorothy Allen, Stella Bowyer, Marjorie Byrne, Ellen Haley, Harry Henshall, Leslie Jessop, Frank Lewis, Connie Palin, Gladys Parry, Annie Parry, Winifred Thompson, Kathleen White, Arthur Whittaker, Betty Hawkins, Myrtle Hawkins, Jack Nelson, Jack Wooliscroft, Walter Wood, Colin Cooper, Clifford Whitehurst, Gladys Norbury and Arthur Owen.

Popular songs of 1944 epitomising the bubbly spirit generated by what was principally good news, were I've Got A Lovely Bunch of Coconuts and the whimsical Mairzy Doats. On New Year's Day, 1945, having been given the day off by the brewery, I took the train to Manchester, walked from London Road station, up Oxford Road to Dover Street and volunteered for the Black Watch Regiment. I was seventeen and a half and had not told my parents of my intentions for to do so would have rendered my aspirations null and void at the very outset. I passed my medical exam easily, was awarded the King's Shilling, and with five other lads celebrated enlistment at a city centre cinema showing 'The Story of Dr Wassal', starring Gary Cooper and Laraine Day. Dad exploded that evening when given the news and came close to apoplexy at the mention of the Black Watch.

"The Black Watch and the Gurkha's are given all the dangerous assignments" he said, "and you are not going to go - I'll see to that!" He did see to it as well but nobody ever came back to me for King George's twelve pence! My act, selfish as it was, was common enough in wartime. I was impetuous, regarded loving bonds as shackles to be unfettered, and felt a need to be liberated. My behaviour leading up to my conscription that year is not something I care to dwell upon for I know I caused pain to those who cared for me and I regret that to this day.

During January a major US invasion of the Philippines was launched by General MacArthur. In the same month Soviet troops liberated the Polish death camp, Auschwitz. In February Tokyo was bombed and 1000 US bombers raided Berlin and British bombers attacked Dresden. The end was surely in sight, confirmed in late April when Italian leader Mussolini and his henchmen were executed and Hitler and Goebels chose suicide as an escape from defeat, humiliation and retribution.

I remember well the morning of May 8th when the end of the Second World War against Germany was officially announced. It was about 10 o'clock and a nice day as I surveyed Park Green from outside my wines and spirits department. There was no sight or sound of celebration, just a quiet serene calm, a fitting end to the hostilities. If I didn't say a prayer at the time, I should have, for I felt tremendous relief - and anger too, that it had all been necessary and had resulted in so much loss of life. I did not then know the cost to Macclesfield - the statistics of 200 lost would come later. We Hunters had been lucky. Tony and Vincent had never reached a combatant stage and we had been spared the deep pain inflicted on other families. Even so, families ostensibly unscathed such as ours, had felt sadness in the mind often enough and often a deeper sense of loss within. Seven young men who have been mentioned previously in my story were such losses. Two lads who had been close to Vincent and me at Central School lost their lives at sea, early in the war. I doubt whether either had reached his eighteenth birthday. Arnold Copeland had volunteered for the Navy, to join his brother, Cyril, who had been at the Co-op Greengrocery department, Sunderland Street. The brothers died together. John Knight had been the school's champion athlete and his spiked running shoes were the first I ever saw.

The other five young men were all flight sergeants in the RAF. Jack, son of Mrs Mullins, the oatcake maker behind the Co-op on Buxton Road; Harry Newton, the Riley-O street game organiser who brought our cinematograph back to life on that dark Sunday evening; Victor Cundiff, the son of our close neighbours in Crew Avenue - his family had already lost eldest son, Maurice, in tragic, non-combatant circumstances earlier in the war; Fred Drinkwater, son of the proprietor of The Little Favourite Shop on Hurdsfield Road who had worked for Holland's, ironmongers; and finally, Jack Bowyer, Tony's pal who played the piano so beautifully for us. Jack Bowyer's loss towards the end of hostilities, was the most painful for my family. Jack was reported 'Missing, believed killed' just three days after giving a sparkling Sunday evening recital on our piano, a stark reminder of how quickly RAF aircrew were thrust into conflict after a brief respite at home.

With the arrival of Barnaby 1945 came my eighteenth birthday and recognition by the Government that I had been Waterloo-boyish long enough and was now required to do a man's job. There was the little matter of the Japanese to attend to and I received my call-up papers and was ordered to report to Richmond, Yorkshire, on Thursday July 19th. Two other pals had the same posting, Eric Sherratt, from the big yard at the end of the Dunbar, a chum throughout my life, and Gerald Thomas, an ex-St George's schoolboy who had shared free school dinners with me at the Pierce Street Clinic.

Our basic training was six weeks. Within that short period, thanks to two very big bombs, the scenario changed dramatically and the Second World War was virtually over. Young men like Eric, Gerald and me could now serve our country with a near certain guarantee that we would be returned to our families in due course, safe and sound.

A terrible price had been paid for such largesse, and for all those who went to war on our behalf - those who returned and those who did not - I cannot resist paraphrasing the memorable words of Laurence Binyon:

> At the going down of the sun and in the morning
> They are all deserving of remembrance.

The marriage of Tony Hunter to Joyce Yomans at St Jame's church, Sutton Lane Ends 25th August 1945. The merging of the Hunter family, left, and the Yomans family, at the end of the War, records a happy conclusion to the book. The author is centre back.